Reconnecting God's Story to Ministry:
Crosscultural Storytelling at Home and Abroad

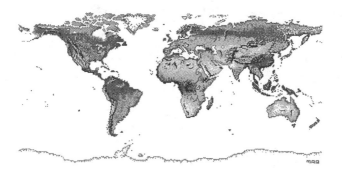

Tom A. Steffen

Foreword by David J.Hesselgrave

Reconnecting God's Story to Ministry:
Crosscultural Storytelling at Home and Abroad

© 1996 by Tom A. Steffen

Published by:

Center for Organizational & Ministry Development
120 East La Habra Blvd., Suite 107
La Habra, CA 90631
Phone: 562/697-6144, 800/604-2663, FAX: 562/691-2081

Unless otherwise noted, all scripture quotations are from the Holy Bible, New International Version. © 1973, 1978, 1984 International Bible Society.

For additional copies contact the above address or

Dr. Tom A. Steffen
Biola University, SICS
13800 Biola Ave
La Mirada, CA 90639
Phone: 562/903-4844; FAX: 562/903-4851;
E-mail: tom_steffen@peter.biola.edu

ISBN 1-882757-03-3

Printed in the United States of America

In memory of

Ruth Marie Steffen

My loving mother, now with the Lord

Contents

Acknowledgments

No work of any worth stands alone. The same is true of *Reconnecting God's Story to Ministry*. I am deeply indebted to many people who helped make this book become a reality. I begin with a special thanks to my mother who introduced me to stories as a young boy. My Sunday School teachers, Helen Kaiser and Evelyn Beer, played major roles in forming a young mind through the stories of characters from the Bible. The Ifugao of the Philippines must receive credit for reintroducing me to the power of stories. Dr. David Hesselgrave receives my great affection for his continuous support and encouragement.

At the School of Intercultural Studies, Biola University, I want to thank the students in the narrative class for their input, especially Elisa (Jansen) Jones, who spent countless hours working over this manuscript. My Biola colleagues, Dr. Judith Lingenfelter and Dr. Don Douglas, deserve a special thanks for their continued encouragement and creative critique. A special thanks goes to Dr. Marvin Mayers who poured over the manuscript, offering countless ideas that now find themselves on the pages.

Foreword

The learned German theologian, Karl Barth, was once asked what he considered to be the most profound truth of Holy Scripture. Without hesitation he replied with the words of a simple gospel song known to every Sunday School child: "Jesus loves me this I know; for the Bible tells me so."

In this book Tom Steffen, in effect, answers a question that in various forms is being asked over and over again in church and mission circles these days: What is the essence of our Christian mission in this world? Steffen's answer can be encapsulated in a variation of the lyrics of one of the most familiar of all Christian hymns: "Tell them the story of Jesus; write on their hearts every word."

But wait a minute! The significance of these answers is not to be found in the answers alone. It is also to be found in the erudition and astuteness of the answers. A biblical example of what I mean is found in the Epistle to the Colossians. In that letter Paul was countering an incipient Gnosticism according to which truth-seekers may needed to attain to elevated knowledge that went far beyond the gospel already communicated to the Christians of Colosse. Paul responded to that heresy with words that well have constituted part of an early Christian "hymn" or, perhaps better, "liturgy." He wrote, "He [Christ] is the beginning, the firstborn from the dead; in order that he might be preeminent in everything; for in him all [God's] fullness was pleased to dwell" (Col. 1:18-19). The truth was that simple! And that profound! But in order to appreciate the simplicity and the profundity of Paul's words, it is important to consider both the breadth of Paul's learning and experience on the one hand and the depth of his teaching and writings on the other.

So it is when it comes to the answers of Karl Barth and Tom Steffen. We may not agree with all of Karl Barth's conclusions, but it is the depth and breadth of the man's learning that lends significance to his assertion that no theological statement transcends the simple truth that Jesus loves us.

As for Tom Steffen, readers should know that he is one of our leading younger missiologists. He has distinguished himself in missionary service in the Philippines, in his teaching career at Biola University, and in his writings. Among the latter, his *Passing the Baton* is one of the finest texts yet available on planting, growing and multiplying the kind of churches that missiologists down through the years have variously described as "indigenous," "responsible," "viable" New Testament churches. *Reconnecting God's Story to Ministry* itself grows out of an extensive knowledge of subject areas absolutely crucial to effective missionizing such as worldview, world religions, contextualization, cross-cultural communication and narrative theology. It provides an in-depth analysis of those critical aspects of fulfilling our Lord's Commission to disciple the world's peoples by more effectively teaching all that He commanded.

It seems to be the case that we Westerners especially have traveled so far down the road of analytical and postulational thinking and communicating that we assume that "good" preaching and teaching will consist of three or four main points, a few subpoints, and one or two illustrations. Stories, we tend to think, are for children. Is it not strange then, that worldviews are largely constructed out of, and communicated by means of, stories of one kind or another? Is it not strange then, that when God Himself wanted to communicate His truth to men and women of all cultures, times and places, He chose to do so by means of one "Big Story"—and many little stories within that "Big Story?"

The fact is that one of the most significant and praise-worthy aspects of modern mission strategy has to do with the re-discovery of the importance of storying the Story of the great redemptive plan of God. No better way of communicating the gospel and discipling the nations has ever been, or ever will be, found. Steffen tells us why this is so and how it is to be done. It is my hope that many will read this book and read it well.

David J. Hesselgrave
Founding Executive Director
Evangelical Missiological Society

Introduction

If stories give meaning to the metaphors / stereotypes / code words / doctrines which we use, then a narrative theology is more fundamental than a propositional theology.
TERRENCE TILLEY

People's assumptions about God impact their perception of Scripture. Those who define the Supreme Being as a God of love may approach Scripture as devotional literature. People who view God as logical and linear may view the Bible as a book of verifiable propositions. Atheists who claim that God does not exist may search the Bible for ways to refute his existence. Some approach the Bible as a great work of literary art, while others use the text mystically to discern direction for life.

My journey into storytelling has been unique. Few of my former colleagues would look in my direction for a book on storytelling. One reason for this is the former way I approached Scripture. I made the Bible a theological textbook. I believed that theology, driven by philosophy and capitalism, was the queen of the sciences. I sank my roots deeply into the argument that the study of textual words and phrases could eventually produce a systematic theology capable of addressing all vital issues of the universe. I defined God as a logical, linear, rational, analytical, and propositional Being interested solely in the minds of people. I built a library that backed my beliefs. Such an unbalanced view of God and Scripture certainly would have made me an unlikely candidate to write a book on storytelling.

A second factor that makes me an unlikely candidate to write this book is that I do not possess the gift of evangelism. I admit frankly that I know of very few people whom I have led to Christ (although several have become effective evangelists). I remember all too well the weekly evangelism assignments in Bible School, when we were required to spend an evening on the street witnessing. I dreaded those evenings. I certainly was not a street preacher, and I hated to approach total strangers. Predictably, I stopped using this evangelism approach as soon as the class was over. This experience left a rather rancid taste in my mouth that poisoned my view of not only street evangelism, but evangelism in general.

Why this book on storytelling? I wrote this book primarily to help readers recapture the most natural, universal, and effective means of evangelism-discipleship that exists—storytelling. The reader will not find an encyclopedic treatise on storytelling—rather, an introductory attempt to reintroduce this lost art. While possessing a rich heritage of storytelling, too many evangelicals have forfeited this vital skill. It's time to reconnect God's story to ministry.

Creative storytelling requires a number of basic skills. This book will introduce practical ways to increase one's storytelling effectiveness in relationship to evangelism-discipleship among those of like culture. While this book should prove helpful to those with the spiritual gift of evangelism, it should prove especially helpful to the majority of us without this gift. I designed this book to assist those who may never participate in formal evangelism, yet wish to honor Christ through verbal testimony. *Reconnecting God's Story to Ministry* will provide such individuals with effective, practical ways to communicate the greatest story ever told.

Today's global village demands that we go further in our training. The culturally diverse cities and towns that surround our churches in North America and other countries demand culturally sensitive stories. Therefore, this book also offers creative tools for crosscultural storytellers at home and abroad. These suggestions should prove applicable for campus workers, trainers of short-termers, apologists, pastors and lay people ministering in culturally diverse communities, and crosscultural Christian workers living in open and restricted access countries.

Storytelling in a different culture creates numerous new pedagogical and theological dynamics, which when gone undetected, can skew the Story. This book moves beyond storytelling in one's own culture to crosscultural storytelling. It will move beyond linear gospel outlines, Western logic and questions, individual responses to traditional evangelism rituals (see for example, Stiles 1995) to a mode of communication that respects the audience, making it easy for them to grasp what they have heard, and to pass it on to others with minimal content loss. Before becoming an effective storyteller in another culture, several roles must precede that of storyteller. A major contribution this book makes is the identification of these roles and the tasks that surround them.

The following questions, that minimize the need for context-specific curricula, highlight one of my concerns for crosscultural storytelling: "Why can't we, via video, use C. Peter Wagner to train thousands of soldiers in local churches worldwide in the areas of church growth and spiritual warfare? Why can't we use Billy Graham, Luis Palau, or Reinhard Bonnke to train people in evangelism? This is exactly the concept we are extending in Nigeria" (Gilfillan 1996:9).

While I believe these men are great trainers, this does not necessarily make them great crosscultural trainers. Those aware of crosscultural communication theory know the above proposal is filled with land mines, of which the trainer may be the last to hear the explosion (or deal with the aftermath). Efficiency often flies in the face of crosscultural training. Wise trainers will forgo such "time savers" because whether by video, oral communication, or written text, the speakers will use different modes of communication, and approach their topics from different worldviews than those of the listeners. Christian workers can ill afford to overlook the need for context-specific stories and curricula. *Reconnecting God's Story to Ministry* takes seriously these differences, and therefore can serve as a practical guide to effective crosscultural storytelling for crosscultural workers.

At this point I would like to state some of my biases in relation to the purpose of this book. *Reconnecting God's Story to Ministry* does not address the various social responsibilities of Christian workers. Even so, I do not consider such activities unimportant or unrelated to the expansion of the Kingdom of God. Our own ministry with the Ifugao of the Philippines included basic medical care and literacy. We did this not only to promote the love of God, but to intentionally assist their transition into the broader national and international communities.

While I will argue aggressively for a return to narrative in evangelism and discipleship, this does not mean I see no need for linear thinking or the systematic presentation of ideas, theological or otherwise. I do not see the issue as an either/or, rather a both/and, with a definite progression. I agree with Hesselgrave and Rommen when they state: "Both the method and content of *biblical* theology must precede the method and content of *systematic* theology when discipling the nations...systematic theology is the crowning, not the foundational, theological type" (1989:214-215).

Some readers may find the terminology used to describe the Bible, such as "story" or "narrative," condescending. Let me assure them of my total commitment to God's word. I become extremely upset when someone tampers with the historical Scriptures "once for all entrusted to the saints" (Jude v.3, New International Version [NIV][1]). Brueggemann captures my sentiments: "Against such an 'emptying' of the stories which Bultmann then 'refills' with modern categories, I propose the stories must be kept in their embarrassing ancientness" (1993:10). I consider all of Scripture inspired by God, capable of leading anyone to saving faith, and unparalleled in value when providing guidance for daily living.

The terms "narrative" and "story" pepper the pages of this book. I use the term "narrative" to refer "in the broadest sense to the account by a narrator of events and participants moving in some pattern over time and space." The word "story" takes a "narrower literary meaning: an account of characters and events in a plot moving over time and space through conflict toward resolution" (Fackre 1984:5).

I designed the book to serve as a bridge between the more popular linear communication mode (presenting subjects logically and sequentially) and the narrative. The reader, therefore, will not find the book communicated in total story format. I hope this introduction to narrative will whet the reader's appetite for additional delicious servings.

Nor will the reader find finished examples of faithstories or Bible stories. These exclusions emphasize the need for each storyteller to create context-specific stories. *Reconnecting God's Story to Ministry* stresses the anthropological, pedagogical, theological, and curricular process over product.

Reconnecting God's Story to Ministry begins by identifying the storylands of key people groups of the Bible, the people group targeted for evangelism-discipleship, and the storyteller. Chapter Two, The Storyanalyst, addresses foundational issues before considering story smithing. Chapters Three and Four call attention to the high concentration of stories found in Scripture (The Storybook), with particular attention given to the Story of stories, the gospel of Jesus Christ (The Storyline). In Chapter Five, I focus on the value of faithstories as a natural, potent evangelistic tool and provide recommendations and a checklist for designing context-specific faithstories (one's faith journey to Christ) and Bible stories. But to become a good storyteller, a number of myths must be overcome. The final two chapters attempt to dispel five myths related to storytelling followed by seven reasons why every Christian worker should become a competent storyteller.

Each chapter closes with probing reflection questions and a helpful bibliography for developing deeper storytelling knowledge, skills, and context-specific curricula.

A story grows out of a culture and a context within that culture (storyland): (1) a fresh and new story, (2) one of their stories reshaped, (3) one of our stories, a Bible story, translated naturally into their language and culture, into another. Wise storytellers will seek to discover the storylands from which stories emerge. Let the journey begin.

[1] All Scripture quotes come from the New International Version unless otherwise stated.

1
The Storylands

> The task of the church is to be faithful to the story of
> God that makes intelligible the divided nature of the world.
> STANLEY HAUERWAS

An advertisement for the Los Angeles Times portrayed the picture of a poor elderly lady on a large billboard. The caption read: "Everyone is a story ready to be told."

No one comes to God's sacred Storybook storyless. The stories constantly retold in a people group's storyland socialize those who live within their socio-cultural boundaries. As Brueggemann correctly points out, these stories typically produce unchallenged worldviews: "By their constant retelling (through propaganda and advertising, or even through parental inculcation), we have come to take these other stories for granted and as "given"" (1993:11).

To reach those living in a specific storyland, the storyteller must be cognizant not only of the land contours of the Bible, but also those of the people group, and especially, his or her own. I will now investigate three foundational storylands.

Scan the Landscapes

Wise communicators of faithstories (personal testimonies) not only want the Storyline (gospel) understood correctly so that transformation (faith-allegiance change) can result, they want listeners to be able to communicate accurately the same message to others. To help accomplish these goals, they will take the necessary time to adequately investigate at least three landscapes: the Bible storylands (Hebrew, Greek, Roman, etc.), the unreached people group's (mariner's) storyland, and the messenger's storyland (see Figure 1).

The Bible Storylands

In that approximately 95 percent of the Bible takes place in 150 miles by 50 miles, storytellers will find it helpful to gain an adequate understanding of the geography and the peoples who populated or traveled through the small country that connects Asia, Africa, and Europe (Egyptians, Philistines, Assyrians, Babylonians, Romans, Greeks). Brueggemann adds another reason for inquiry: "[in the Bible] land is never simply physical dirt but is always physical dirt with social meanings derived from historical experience" (1977:2). While it is impossible to cover such a broad topic in detail in this brief section, I will merely highlight several foundational areas that storytellers can build upon through commentaries and other sources. This first considers Israel's socio-cultural progression over time.[1]

The original Israelites were nomadic bands consisting of extended family alliances (patrilocal), e.g. Abraham, Isaac, Jacob, Laban. Abraham, the first Israelite, was a wealthy caravanner who no doubt had covenant

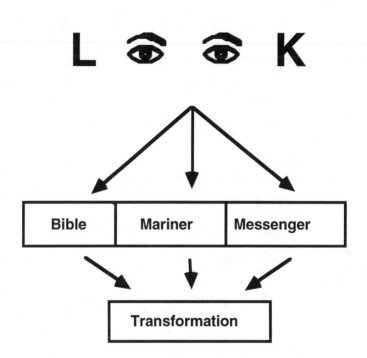

Figure 1. Scanning the landscapes

relationships with the heads of far flung villages so that he could sell his merchandise and animals uncontested. The early Israelites believed God owned the land and worshipped him collectively, led by the family patriarch.

Escaping from Egypt, tribal Israel moved into the Promised Land and took up a new role, pastoralists. Living in villages and walled towns, family clans competed for land for agricultural and husbandry purposes. Division of labor produced different economic classes: the wealthy and the poor. Orphans and widows became classic victims of an economic system based on land and patriarchal leadership. God therefore instructed the Israelites not to harvest the corners of the fields so that the poor would have a source of food (Lev. 19:9; Ruth 2:1-3). Should outside forces invade the land, warlords, such as Joshua or another judge, would call together the segmentary alliances to fight the advancing intruder. Once the battle was won, survivors returned to pastoral activities. Annual worship ceremonies led by priests and prophets concerned with crop and animal fertility, illnesses, and so forth, centered around the tabernacle.

In time, Israel chose to become a city-state under King Saul. Villages became fortified cities with bureaucracy, records, militaries, international debt, and, the inevitable, taxes. Occupations became much more specialized: weavers, potters, carpenters, soldiers, tax collectors. Priests became appointees of the king, overseeing the centralized worship institutionalized in the capital city to follow the annual calendar of religious and political events.

Moving to the New Testament, Jewish family structure continued, influenced by its tribal, peasant, and kingdom heritage (Lingenfelter 1992:128). Trade guilds influenced labor practices, helping to protect the widows and orphans. Worship remained centralized in the Jerusalem temple led by professional priests, along with synagogues that dotted the countrysides. The Sanhedrin, operating out of the temple, served as Israel's supreme court. A number of Jewish sects expressed various ideologies: Essenes, Pharisees, Sadducees, Herodians, Zealots, Scribes.

With the Assyrians and Babylonians in their past, Israel now lived under the arresting influence of the Romans and Greeks. And like their ancestors in the Old Testament, some came under the influence of competing worldviews. For instance, some of the Colossians developed a protognosticism, a syncretistic blend of Judaism, oriental mysticism, and Greek philosophy. They reacted to this combination of special passwords, secret knowledge, astrology, angels, visions, rituals, regulations in one of two ways: asceticism or antinomianism. Using key terms ("hidden," "knowledge," "mystery," "wisdom") that would strike home, Paul rebuked the Colossians with a sharp letter. He argued that true believers will give the resurrected Christ his rightful preeminence, and because they have access to *complete* spiritual knowledge, they must demonstrate transformed behavior, i.e. actions that will glorify Christ, not the defeated subservient powers.

Storytellers who want to communicate effectively with a specific people group will make sure they have an adequate understanding of the different Bible landscapes. This knowledge will allow them to provide a scenery backdrop (history, setting, context) for the Bible stories so that truth walks onto the stage with meaning. Such a background will also help assure that the listeners will grasp the socio-cultural distinctives of stories coming from different time periods in Israel's history: tribal, peasant, kingdom, Palestine, Greco-Roman, making it less likely to add extra biblical material. But we cannot stop here: wise storytellers will also want to investigate the unreached people group's (mariner's) storyland.

The Mariner's Storyland

A mariner can be defined as an unbelieving member of a people group adrift spiritually on the seas of life in search of a safe harbor in which to drop anchor. These individuals have a "God-shaped vacuum;" their heart, says St. Augustine, "is restless, until it repose in Thee."

Larson (1978) objects to those storytellers who would enter a mariner's storyland and immediately begin to tell Bible stories or his or her own faithstory without first scanning the mariner's storyland. He argues that mariners view such encounters as either a schoolhouse, a market place, or a courtroom. When in school, the messenger becomes the teacher while they become the students. When at the market place, the messenger becomes the seller while they become the buyer. When in the courtroom, the messenger becomes the accuser while they become the accused.

Larson asks rhetorically: "Can an outsider teach or sell or accuse an insider?" (p.157) He then sets forth a healthier role sequence: learner before teacher, buyer before seller, accused before accuser. Beginning with the learner role soon leads to the trader role. When the mariner perceives that the messenger is truly serious about learning his or her language and culture, the trader role emerges. As messengers trade information with the mariner, the role of storyteller follows naturally. Having earned the right to be heard, the storyteller now proceeds to tell Bible stories to friends.

While Larson's article focuses on language learning, I would like to adapt it more specifically to reconnecting God's story to ministry. Messengers would take the following roles: learner[2] (of the mariner's lifestories), trader (of lifestories from around the world), storyteller (of ideas and images, events and characters, faithstories [Chapter 5]). This role sequence calls for the messenger to enter the mariner's storyland with the express purpose of learning his or her lifestories *before* becoming a storyteller. It demands the messenger earn the right to be heard *before* beginning ministry, so that when stories are told, they are told to friends. This approach brings credibility not only to the storyteller, but also to the stories told.

Collect lifestories. One way to gain an understanding of the mariner's worldview is to collect a generous number of lifestories from different age groups and genders.[3] Bertaux warns about collecting too few lifestories:

> While social research needs to use a variety of sources in order to observe as fully as possible a given 'object', this object should never be an individual as such but rather a sociological object; that is, a given set of social relations. In this perspective it seems necessary to collect not one but several life stories; and this contributes to solving the problem of truthfulness as these life stories may be 'checked' against each other, as far as matters of sociological interest are concerned (private matters becoming irrelevant of the sociologist) (1981:8-9).

When collecting lifestories, messengers would seek specific data on family, friends, housing, economics, lifecycle, community, religion, culture change, and so forth. A cultural analysis of each lifestory collected would follow, producing a general cultural picture of the people group. Bertaux's point is well taken:

> The analysis of life histories does not primarily aim at individual particularities, but seeks to unravel what general (or generalizable) elements they contain. By representing individual life histories, the biographical method is meant to give access to the reality of life of social aggregates (strata, classes, cultures, etc.) (1981:63).

Collect proverbs. Proverbs express the values of a people. Wise messengers will collect proverbs and attempt to isolate the values espoused. Consider the values expressed in these Mid-Eastern proverbs: "My brother and I against my cousin, my cousin and I against a stranger." "A man is known by his manners not his clothes." Proverbs provide messengers with key insights into how the mariner views the world. The messenger could tie such proverbs to proverbs from the Storybook along with Bible stories that relate the same message.

Analyze storytelling from the mariner's perspective. Another way to learn the mariner's storyland in relation to storytelling is to investigate their use of stories in formal (school, church, government), non-formal (planned seminars, conferences), and informal (casual, spontaneous gatherings) settings (see Table 1). Knowing if the setting is formal, nonformal or informal, the type of event, who can tell stories, the dress attire required of the storyteller, the length of stories, character development, the themes, values, felt needs, emotions expressed in the stories, the type of relationships contrasted in the stories, the paraphernalia used, who attends, floor ethics, and the style of the story presentation can go a long way in preparing messengers to become effective storytellers in a specific storyland. Contrasting the results of the above analysis with that of the Bible's storylands should prove helpful in identifying the socio-cultural bridges, barriers, and information gaps. Again, the wise messenger will not stop here, but will seek to contrast his or her own storyland with those of the Bible and the mariner.

The Messenger's Storyland

Of the three landscapes, probably the most difficult to really know is one's own. Community stories on the formal, non-formal and informal levels smith and shape personal stories to such an extent that they become normal (which tends to make all differing stories abnormal). Bellah unfolds this thought further:

> People growing up in communities of memory not only hear the stories that tell how the community came to be, what its hopes and fears are, and how its ideals are exemplified by outstanding men and women; they also participate in the practices—rituals, aesthetic, ethical—that defined the community as a way of life (1985:154).

Know the messenger's history. Knowing one's past can help one know his or her present. For example, for many Americans, the conquering pioneer spirit of the frontier days has helped mold contemporary values. The early European settlers found before them a vast, rich land, seemingly open for the taking. But the conquering of this land was fraught with dangers: climatic, defiant residents, ignorance, and so forth. These very dangers and challenges, however, helped create a people that valued pragmatism, rugged individualism, teamwork, freedom, expansionism, siding with the underdog, speed, efficiency, informality, survival of the fittest, restlessness, self-reliance, privacy, voluntarism, conquering new frontiers, and an optimistic future (the "American Dream").

Add to the above values a sense of spiritual mission. The new settlers believed God sent them as a covenanted people to inaugurate a new period of history (Dyrness 1989:63). They envisioned God and country as one; therefore, an attack on them (God's people) was considered an attack on God, and therefore doomed to fail.

Table 1

Storytelling Analysis Worksheet

	Formal	Nonformal	Informal
Event (purpose)			
Place			
Storyteller(s)			
Gender			
Dress			
Time (start to finish)			
Character development			
Themes			
Values rewarded / rejected			
Needs expressed			
Emotions expressed			
Relationships contrasted			
Paraphernalial			
Attendees			
Floor ethics			
Story style			

The ancestors of these pioneering people would develop four sports that would continue to epitomize the foundational values: baseball, basketball, American football, and a new Olympic event, beach volleyball. The four sports also serve as microcosms of the nation. For instance, the sport of baseball depicts labor-management relations, a player's individual effort in relation to the team effort, the need for rules, regulations, and enforcers (umpires), family recreation and food (hot dogs and popcorn), philosophy of winning/losing,[4] racism, sexism, and nationalism (each game begins with the national anthem). Every game played, in any of the these sports, reviews and reinforces key American values to all who participate or observe.

Discern the messenger's social environments. Not only is it helpful for the messenger to know his or her values, and contrast them with those of the mariners, it is also helpful for them to know and contrast social environments. Lingenfelter (1992; 1996) has designed a grid/group model for discovering the emphasis given the social environments of property, labor, exchange, family authority, community authority, conflict and political interests, ritual, and cosmology. Messengers will find it helpful to know which of the five social "ways of life" (individual, collectivist, corporate, bureaucratic, hermit) they find for each of the social environments. Plotting one's social environments, and then contrasting them to those of the mariner and selected Bible stories, will not only reveal socio-cultural differences and similarities, it will also provide guidance for designing a single story or series of stories.

Conclusion

Taking the time to scan the three cultural landscapes leads us to conclude that no person is storyless, and that everyone's story should be heard with empathy. Such research will help address some of the most overlooked questions in evangelism (Chapter 4). It will also establish the price tag each cultural landscape assigns to values and worldview assumptions. And it helps those hearing the stories to repeat them in a manner that protects the integrity of Scripture.

But there is more. Before becoming an effective storyteller, one must become a storyanalyst.

[1] I am indebted to Sherwood Lingenfelter for many of these insights.

[2] Some contexts may require that you relate your lifestory first.

[3] See Steffen's *Passing the Baton* 1993, Chapter 8, for a comprehensive cultural analysis model along with culture learning levels.

[4] A study of the philosophy of winning in sports seems to demonstrate a change over time; from "it's how you play the game" to Vince Lombardi's "Winning is everything!" to the present day "in your face" humiliation.

Reflection:

What new questions does this chapter raise for you?

Which storyland do you know best? Least?

What ministry changes do you anticipate making?

For Further Reading:

Brueggemann, Walter
1977   The Land: Place as Gift, Promise, and Challenge in Biblical Faith. Philadelphia: Fortress Press.
Lingenfelter, Sherwood G.
1992   Transforming Culture: A Challenge for Christian Mission. Grand Rapids, MI: Baker Book House.
1996   Agents of Transformation: A Guide for Effective Cross-cultural Ministry. Grand Rapids, MI: Baker Book House.
Lingenfelter, Sherwood G. and Marvin K. Mayers
1986   Ministering Cross-Culturally: An Incarnational Model for Personal Relationships. Grand Rapids, MI: Baker Book House.
Keener, Craig S.
1995   The IVP Bible Background Commentary: New Testament. Downers Grove, IL: InterVarsity Press.
Mayers, Marvin K.
1987   Christianity Confronts Culture: A Strategy for Crosscultural Evangelism. Grand Rapids, MI: Zondervan Publishing House.
Stewart, Edward C. and Milton J. Bennett
1991   American Cultural Patterns: A Cross-Cultural Perspective. Yarmouth, ME: Intercultural Press, Inc.

2
The Storyanalyst

Only one generation separates a
heritage remembered from a heritage forgotten.
LEROY FORD

...if evangelization is more about communication between
living people, about the uttering of a living word, about the
incarnation of the word in culture, and about an urgent and
vibrant call to action, then orality certainly needs to be
reexamined as a possible vehicle. And even if we remain
unconvinced that literacy should be undenied, we could
consider the enhanced empowerment of ourselves and the
recipients of evangelization that would result from a missionary
approach employing *both* literacy *and* orality as resources.
ANTHONY GITTINS

The crowds who heard Jesus "were amazed at his
teaching, because he taught as one who had authority"
(Matt. 7:28, 29)! The guards declared, "No one ever spoke
the way this man does" (Jn. 7:46). After Peter finished
speaking, "they were cut to the heart," asking "What shall
we do?" (Acts 2:37) Paul's comments caused Felix and
Agrippa to tremble (Acts 24:25; 26:28). What can
storyanalysts (those who investigate the storylands) do to
help elicit such responses from the mariner?

Few messengers have received intentional training for telling Bible stories or faithstories. As I reflect back over my own training, I received less than minimal training in these areas. If the story genre is as important as God seems to indicate by its extensive use in the sacred Storybook, it seems this is a gross miscalculation by those in positions to influence training in mono- or crosscultural settings. Are Christian trainers (and hence the majority Christian populous) neglecting one of the most powerful modes of communication available? Why do believers tend to neglect this genre while many unbelievers rely heavily upon it? Metz (in Hauerwas and Jones 1989) makes this disturbing observation:

> They [marginal groups and religious sects] tell the story of their conversion and retell biblical stories, sometimes in a patently helpless way that is open to manipulation....Are these marginal groups not in fact drawing on something that has for too long been hidden and neglected in Christianity, its narrative potential? Are they not remembering that Christians do not primarily form an argumentative and reasoning community, but a story-telling community, and that the exchange of experiences of faith, like that of any "new" experience, takes a narrative form (pp. 254-255)?

To help evoke similar responses received by Jesus, Peter, Paul, not to mention the numerous marginal groups noted by Metz, I will now consider four categories in relation to the storylands of the Bible, the messenger, and the mariner discussed in the previous chapter: the anthropological, the pedagogical, the theological, and the curricular. Before discussing the four, I will note several foundational issues.

Foundational Considerations

Clancy's (1993) statement snapped me to attention: "The most difficult initial problem in the history of literacy is appreciating what preceded it." Before residing among the Ifugao of the Philippines I had little appreciation for oral communication. As one trained for a lifetime in literacy, I felt oral communication could never match the superior strengths offered by written communication. I had fallen into the trap Clancy describes.

Somehow I had failed to appreciate that it was God's powerful words that brought the universe into being, that most people were illiterate during Old and New Testament times, calling for the public reading of Scripture (Neh. 8:8-9; 1 Tim. 4:13; Rev. 1:3), that saving faith comes by hearing (Rom. 10:17), that blessing or cursing someone verbally really works. "Sound," argues Ong, "unites groups of living beings as nothing else does"(1981:122). Kelber goes further:

> Spoken words breathe life, drawing their strength from sound. They carry a sense of presence, intensity, and instantaneousness that writing fails to convey....They address hearers directly and engage them personally in a manner unattainable by the written medium (1983:18-19).

One of the reasons I had failed to give oral stories the credit they deserve was because I had overlooked the power resident in oral communication, something God did not.

At this point it may prove helpful to distinguish the relation between story, myth, history and worldview. Worldview, the linguistic-cultural assumptions and presuppositions that distinguish one people group from another and form subcultures within, finds its foundational meaning in myths and stories. Myths and stories convey their message through historical or fictional characters and beings, sometimes rationally, sometimes in contradictory ways. They are communicated orally, in written prose or on the screen. Those not found in print or picture change over time as legitimate and illegitimate contextualization takes place.[1] Nevertheless, these two powerful genres form, warn, heal, and transform every worldview, whether Islamic, Hindu, Buddhist, Judaism, scientific, or Christian. To survive, any worldview requires the recitation of myths and stories.

To change a people group's worldview requires the hearing and/or seeing of different stories. To change a people group's worldview so that Christ becomes central requires the hearing and/or seeing of stories from Scripture. Unlike some myths and stories, Bible stories find themselves rooted in history and the Supernatural. Their authenticity stands the test of time and legitimate contextualization. Through these powerful stories and our faithstories (which connect to them), the Holy Spirit transforms the worldviews of people and communities.

Assembling a storyteam begins the worldview change process of a people group uncommitted to Christ. Identify the storytellers and curricula writers, both nationals and expatriates so that multi-perspectives receive appropriate attention initially and continually. Convene the group to discuss purpose and direction, making sure individual expectations become clear to all.

Request Holy Spirit involvement *throughout* the project. Storyanalysts will want the assistance of the greatest Storyanalyst of all, the Holy Spirit. Those who demonstrate dependency on the Holy Spirit will receive the supernatural help required for this spiritual endeavor.

Conduct a joint job analysis. Who is the mariner (age, gender, subculture)? What does the unbelieving mariner need to know / do / be to become a believer? What do new believers need to be able to know / do / be to face family members, cults, critics? The joint job analysis will provide the storyteam with foundational information for content and design inclusions in the individual faithstories and Bible story series.

Connect the faithstories and Bible stories with the life stories of the mariners. Powell observes: "Readers are most likely to empathize with characters who are similar to them (realistic empathy) or with characters who represent what they would like to be (idealistic empathy)" (1990:56). Tilley adds: "a story is true to the extent that it re-presents our world or part of it in a revealing way" (1985:188). Captivating stories reflect characters and characteristics that the mariner can identify.

Any story which we adopt, or allow to adopt us, argue Hauerwas & Burrell, will have to display four qualities:

(1) power to release us from destructive alternatives;
(2) ways of seeing through current distortions;
(3) room to keep us from having to resort to violence;
(4) a sense for the tragic: how meaning transcends power
    (in Hauerwas & Jones 1989:185).

Storyanalysts will want to investigate stories for the above inclusions. (This is best accomplished through the formation of a storyteam [Chapter 6].) Faithstories and Bible stories that connect culturally (individually and communally) will carry the ring of truth that lead to Truth. Such stories will challenge existing worldviews, laying the foundation for personal and communal transformation to Christ.

Smithing A Four-Legged Story

Because of the placement and balanced support provided by a four-legged stool, users find it difficult to turn over. In a similar sense, stories that consider the anthropological, pedagogical, theological, and curricular legs of a story make it much more difficult for the mariner to upset (miss) its intended meaning. Investigating the four legs of the story will help the storyanalysts provide the mariner with a culturally and theologically sound story.

To ensure culturally and theologically sound stories, storyanalysts must consider the four legs of the story from two other perspectives besides their own: the mariner's and the message's. Diligent storyteams triangulate the study of the four-legs study to include the three perspectives of messenger, message, and mariner. While such a study requires extra time and expense, the outcomes far surpass those of imported curriculum designed for another audience. Every people group deserves to hear God's stories in their own language and culture (Acts 2:11).

The Anthropological Leg

The anthropological leg of the stool respects the mariner's worldview, values, and social environments. This leg of the stool requires the storyanalysts to take sufficient time not only to learn the mariner's culture, but become competent participants in it. It demands that relationships not only be built, but built with the right people.

Every time someone tells a story, in some way and at some level, crosscultural communication occurs. The storyanalysts, therefore, must also be cognizant of their own worldviews, values, and social environments. The same holds true for the various cultures highlighted in the sacred Storybook (see Figure 1, p.17). Like the stage crew for a Shakespearean play, the storyteam provides the backdrop, sets the scenery with history, setting and context, so that when Truth walks on the stage, so will biblical meaning. The anthropological studies of these areas of the storyanalyst, the mariner, and the Bible culture covered in the story will go a long ways in smithing stories that culturally and theologically connect.

The Pedagogical Leg

The pedagogical leg of the stool respects the mariner's learning styles. This leg of the stool requires the storydesigners to learn the mariner's preferred way to learn, store, and retrieve information on the formal, nonformal, and informal levels (see Table 1, p.24).

Storyanalysts must also be cognizant of their own preferred learning styles. In that we often teach as we were taught, storyanalysts in their naiveté frequently take for granted that if they learned something in a particular way, so can anyone else. Mistake. To illustrate, the Japanese *TV Guide* provides readers with the plot and outcome of a movie. The editors leave no room for suspense in these areas. The Japanese consider the group response to an act of greatest importance (discovery process), not who did what to whom, which many readers of this book would prefer.

Storyanalysts will not want to overlook the emphasis God gives to the various genres in the Storybook. While all genres have a place in learning (demonstrating God's unique diversity), the sacred Storybook gives tremendous emphasis to narrative (see Figure 10, p.125). The author of the sacred Storybook is well aware of the power of human experience (archetypes) that transcends cultures and generations.

The Theological Leg

The theological leg of the stool respects the mariner's religious beliefs and practices. This leg of the stool requires the storyanalysts to grasp the mariner's understanding of the supernatural, covering the entire life cycle as defined by the mariner. Such a study may bring to light theological categories hitherto overlooked by the storyanalysts, such as dreams, demons, deliverances, healings, ancestor worship, polygamy, community, mentorship, justice, poverty, persecution, secularism, materialism, and so forth. It will no doubt give fundamental doctrines related to the gospel (the Storyline) different definitions. To illustrate, sin may be defined as laziness or stinginess rather than missing the mark. After death destinations may not include heaven or hell. I believe it was D.J. Bosch who astutely observed: "We usually know exactly what we have gone to give to people...We do not know as clearly what we have gone to receive."

As in the prior two legs of the story, the storyanalysts will want to investigate their understanding of the key components of the Storyline, recognizing the powerful influence of worldview. As the storyanalysts seek to guard the gospel, they will intentionally explore the sacred Storybook in search of theologies as culture-free as possible, acknowledging no one can interpret the sacred Storybook cultureless! Storyanalysts will reflect on competing interpretations, recognizing that the sacred Storybook read in community (past and present) will help point out cultural blind spots. All theologies must be as deHebrewized, deHellenized, deWesternized and denationalized as possible.

Storyanalysts that desire worldview transformation (for all parties) will investigate theological categories and doctrinal definitions in search of cultural limitations imposed by worldview. To accomplish this, they will investigate both Testaments, conceding the need for the complete counsel of God. "Worldview change is best accomplished," argues Hesselgrave, "by studying and telling or retelling the biblical big story that enshrines the Christian worldview" (1994:50). Biblical theology can assist them in this endeavor.

The Curricular Leg

The curricular leg of the stool respects the mariner's preference for the sequencing and formatting of written and taped (video and cassette) materials. This leg of the stool requires the storyanalysts to ponder what the mariner prefers in relation to discourse and design features: introductions and closings; body; characters introduced, traced, and exited; implicit and explicit information; questions; logic; illustrations; themes; application; flow; sequence; integration; length; depth; format; size; color and so forth.

Storyanalysts will want to reflect on the particulars of curricula from the mariner's perspective. What do the storyanalysts consider good curricula? How does this differ from that of the mariner? How does this differ from that laid out in the sacred Storybook? What will happen to the curricula should the "big picture" narrative of the sacred Storybook be lost? How will the storyanalysts adjust the curricula so that it is comprehensive (covers both

Testaments, ties together evangelism and follow-up), contextual (connects culturally), confrontational (challenges worldview and current faith allegiance), calls for immediate, practical application, and reproducible (storied with minimal loss of meaning) by those who interact with it?

In summary, should storyanalysts decide to overlook (intentionally or naively) the investigation of any of the four legs of the stool from the three perspectives of messenger, message, and mariner, they do so at great peril. Such an oversight demonstrates lack of respect for the mariner, not to mention blatant ethnocentrism. It also jeopardizes the understanding and proliferation of the standard Storyline of the sacred Storybook.

Conclusion

Storyanalysts have the distinct privilege of learning about others and themselves *before* becoming storytellers. They recognize that time spent in this capacity is as much ministry as evangelizing and discipling. They also will learn there is no universal way to tell a story, but rather there are better ways. Therefore, they take the time necessary to investigate the four legs of the story stool from the three perspectives of messenger, message, and mariner. Their efforts often become rewarded when they elicit the same responses received by Jesus, Peter, Paul, and yes, the marginal groups. Faithstories and Bible stories transform worldviews.

Our understanding of the Bible is often fragmented. Is the Bible a collection of isolated stories? This question will now be considered.

[1] See chapter 10 of Hesselgrave and Rommen (1989) for an excellent discussion on revelational epistemology.

Reflection:

What new questions does this chapter raise for you?

What role do myths and stories play in the development and transformation of worldview?

Why should one analyze the target audience and himself or herself before beginning to tell stories?

Are your stories comprehensive? Contextual? Confrontational? Do they call for practical, immediate application? Are they reproducible?

What ministry changes do you anticipate making?

For Further Reading:

Kraft, Charles K.
    1991   Communication Theory for Christian Witness. NY: Orbis
            Books.
Hiebert, Paul G.
    1985   Anthropological Insights for Missionaries. Grand Rapids,
            MI: Baker Book House.
    1995   Incarnational Ministry: Planting Churches in Band, Tribal,
            Peasant, and Urban Societies. Grand Rapids, MI: Baker
            Book House.
Ong, Walter J.
    1982   Orality and Literacy: Technologizing of the Word. New
            York: Methuen.
Tonkin, Elizabeth
    1992   Narrating Our Pasts: The Social Construction of Oral
            History. (Studies in Oral and Literate Cultures: No.22)
            N.Y: Cambridge University Press.

3
The Storybook

The fundamental mode of Scripture is story.
DONALD MILLER

The Christian Story met the
mythological search for romance by being a story
and the philosophical search for truth by being a true story.
G.K. CHESTERTON

For many inside and outside the community of faith, the Bible has become a book of isolated stories rather than a unified Storybook. They often view the Book as a multitude of fragmented stories rather than one coherent Story. Like a lone diamond, each Bible story retains its own beauty and quality; yet like a tennis bracelet, each can increase its individual value dramatically when linked together with the other stories. This chapter will explore the unified nature of the Bible, God's Storybook.

A Fragmented Storybook

Biblical illiteracy continues to grow among believers in the United States. Barna points out in a recent survey that "only 4 out of every 10 adults will read any portion of the Bible outside the church during the week" (1993:48). The researcher goes on to paint an ominous picture:

> Lay members are abysmally ignorant of the basics of the Bible. Most cannot name half of the Ten Commandments. Most people do not know that it was Jesus Christ who preached the Sermon on the Mount. Ask about the book of Thomas, and nearly half of all adults will be unaware that such a book is not in the Bible (1993:48-49).

Such biblical illiteracy leads to a fragmented understanding of the Bible. Believers exposed to the Bible find few unifying themes that tie pertinent characters and truths together. They often find little consistency between the two Testaments.

If such fragmentation exists among believers, how much more among those outside the community of faith? Sue Miller, director of Willow Creek Community Church's program for children from birth to fifth grade, observes: "To assume that they [the young students] can jump into the middle of a traditional curriculum is naive" (Midgett 1993:45). This young population lacks a clear grasp of Bible fundamentals. One wonders if those ministering to different generations or nationalities will find things that different. Besides a lack of exposure to the sacred Storybook, what causes such a fragmented understanding of the Bible?

Causes of Fragmentation

For many, God's sacred Storybook has become a myriad of isolated characters and themes. While there are numerous reasons for such outcomes, I will attempt to identify several that often go unnoticed.

The printing press has been extremely influential in promoting fragmentation as it brought text to the general public. With the advent of moveable print (Gutenberg) came lines of print that the eyes follow across the page (for Westerners), down a line, and back across the page. This seemingly innocent exercise promotes linear thought as it trains the mind to build from one thought to the next intuitively. The printed text also allows for the extraction and analysis of words and phrases, often causing the whole to become lost in the parts. The printed sequence of words, along with the ideas they promote, have fueled fragmentation. A natural progression follows.

During the Reformation, editors introduced chapters and verses to the Bible text. This numerical grid imposed upon the Bible text facilitated quick reference. Hard-to-find segments of Scripture soon became much more accessible and distinguishable. With the passing of time, many mistakenly assumed this powerful tool to be part of the original manuscripts. From their perspective, God delivered the sacred Story in natural chapters and verses.

Under the influence of this numerical grid, Bible study methodology changed dramatically. No longer did Bible teachers have to guess where an author's point began or ended; the predetermined chapters and verses did this for them automatically. Teachers could now begin a study at any point in the document simply by stating: "Let's turn

to chapter..." or more specifically, "Let's turn to chapter
...., verse...."

Focused textual Bible study allowed for self-contained verses to evolve, e.g., "Train up a child..."
(Prov. 22:6). Entire sermons or lessons could flow from a
single verse, supported by multiple biblical cross-references. Memorization of the self-contained verse(s)
provided the necessary theological validation for any
topic. Proof texting followed naturally.

Numerous Bible study tools such as dictionaries,
commentaries, and chain-reference Bibles rolled off the
presses, feeding the fragmentation of the sacred
Storybook. With a ready reference system of chapters and
verses, theologians could focus attention on easily
identifiable words and phrases. Readers of their
publications received extensive insights into the minute
details of how a word was constructed in the original
language. But how these intricate details influenced the
entire text often received inadequate attention from
teachers.

Bible translators used the numerous Bible study
commentaries and aids to produce exegetical helps
(commentary compilations of key information for each
verse of individual books of the Bible). The production of
exegetical helps saved translators around the world from
reinventing the research wheel. No longer would each
translator have to do extensive study to find out the
meaning of phrases or words. The exegetical helps
allowed them to focus extra time on Bible translation.

Initially, like many Bible study tools, the exegetical
helps focused primarily on the interpretation of key words
and phrases. Also, like many Bible study helps, they
tended to overlook the literary styles of the books and
letters being translated.

The translation of the New Testament alone has done much to fragment the understanding of Scripture for many people groups. Providing readers the last section of Scripture presents a truncated story. Bible translators who try to rectify this problem later by providing Old Testament sections will certainly help the situation, but once a foundation is laid, it becomes very difficult for the recipients to unify the two.

Bible training institutes often promote fragmentation. In my own case, word studies and systematic theology predominated in the classes I attended. Teachers often taught books of the Bible "verse-by-verse." Key words in passages began a hopscotch journey through the Bible in search of parallel passages. The collective use of a word from Genesis to Revelation set the parameters for interpretation. How all this related to the human author's intent of the books for a particular audience often went overlooked. Systematic theology provided the "whole" of a topic, but rarely told how the whole topic fit into God's total program.

While my individual classes were often fragmented, missions served as a unifying theme for all the curricula. Dedicated Bible teachers taught me God's mission agenda from Alpha to Omega. I learned to process all theology through this mission grid. But not every Bible student has this luxury. David Wells captures the feelings of many Bible students when he addresses the fragmentation of knowledge within the seminary curriculum:

> Subjects and fields develop their own working assumptions, vocabularies, technical terms, criteria for what is true and false, and canons of what literature and what views should be common knowledge among those working in the subjects. The result of this is a profound increase in knowledge but often an equally profound loss in understanding what it all means, how the knowledge in one field should inform that in another. This

is the bane of every seminarian's existence. The disassociated fields—biblical studies, theology, church history, homiletics, ethics, pastoral psychology, missiology—become a rain of hard pellets relentlessly bombarding those who are on the pilgrimage to graduation. Students are left more or less defenseless as they run this gauntlet, supplied with little help in their efforts to determine how to relate the fields one to another. In the end, the only warrant for their having to endure the onslaughts is that somehow and someday it will all come together in a church (1993:244-245).

Besides the lack of exposure to biblical truth, as well as the reasons listed above, other explanations for a fragmented understanding of the Bible exist. These could include the Western bifurcated view of the material and spiritual worlds, as well as learning style, e.g., the preference of many Westerners to begin learning about the individual parts, before considering the whole. I will now reflect on the fallout of fragmentation.

Fallout of Fragmentation

A fragmented grasp of the Bible often results in some people missing the big picture. Caught up in the details of minutia, Bible students often fail to see God's overall plan. With many teachers and commentators focusing attention on words, parts of words, phrases, or paragraphs, the human author's overall intent often becomes obscured. At a broader level, individual books may take on spurious meanings unsupported by the "whole will of God." Commentators and teachers frequently overlook how individual books fit into the scheme of the 66 books of the Bible. This often causes students to overlook the unified themes of the Storybook. Biblical and narrative theologies become stepsisters to systematic theology.

Another result of the fragmentation of Scripture is that some people tend to develop theological categories of convenience, i.e. theologies that address the needs and concerns of particular worldviews. These speculative theologies often emerge based on culturally influenced selections of isolated texts. Holy history sometimes takes a subservient role to personal and/or communal histories. Local expressions of Scripture tend to take precedence over global interpretations over the centuries. For example, Western theology tends to emphasize Scripture sections that highlight individualism, the immediate family, time-management, fairness, and so forth. Such theologies, born in certain time periods by people facing particular challenges, often become static, even as advocates promote them around the world as the complete packet of universal truth. Again, often lost to the process is the critical critique of the Storybook's "whole will of God."

People influenced by other worldviews often highlight theologies minimized by Westerners. For example, some emphasize texts that deal with the supernatural, dreams, angels and demons, extended family and genealogies, ancestor worship, community, corporate sin, justice from oppressors, and so forth. Worldviews influence the development of theological categories of convenience which automatically create blinders to other themes of the Storybook.

A third result of fragmentation of the Storybook is the lack of attention paid to the literary genres of the sacred texts. Rather than treat each document as a particular piece of literature scripted for a specific audience and time, teachers and students often impose the use of exegetical tools that violate the literary nature of the text. Literary genres, narrative being the predominant (see Figure 10, p.125), often find themselves sacrificed on the altar of isolated, abstract propositions. Sadly, this scenario perpetuates itself around the world because teachers tend to teach others as they were taught.

The fragmentation of the Storybook tends to produce Christian workers who separate evangelism from effective follow-up (ongoing teaching and mentoring that result in responsible members of a community of faith). Witnesses for Christ often begin the gospel presentation in the middle of the Storybook, the Gospels. They see little need to provide a firm foundation for the gospel message. Those accepting Christ as Savior are often sent on their way, encouraged to read the Book of John and associate with those of like faith. For many, a great gulf exists between evangelism and ongoing follow-up.

Believers who witness tend to overlook the need to front-load the gospel message with sufficient Scripture so that a solid foundation of the "Good News" is laid. They also fail to see how such foundational teaching provides solid groundwork for the eventual instruction of new believers. Without such an instructional background, our present evangelistic methodologies often produce a host of "professing believers" that mar the character of Christ and Christianity. Because our understanding of the Storybook tends to be piecemeal, Jesus' command to "make disciples," i.e. evangelism that results in obedient members of the community of faith, often remains piecemeal. Recipients usually witness as they were taught to witness.

A Unified Storybook

God's Storybook presents a unified story (see Figure 2). This integration allows its readers and listeners to grasp the big picture, expand traditional theological categories of convenience, respect the literary genres of the Storybook, and wed evangelism to follow-up.

Grasps the Big Picture

The sacred Storybook presents God's story to the world. Analyzing the narrative unity found within the Old Testament, Fee and Stuart (1993:79-81) identified three levels of stories: (1) the *top level,* which addresses the universal plan of God, or "redemptive history." Key aspects of the plot include Creation, the Fall, the power of pervasiveness of sin, the need for redemption, and Christ's incarnation and sacrifice. (2) The *middle level* centers on Israel: the call of Abraham, the Abrahamic lineage, the enslaving of Israel in Egypt, God's deliverance of Israel from bondage, Israel's conquest of the Promised Land, disobedience, God's protection and pleading to Israel, the destruction of Northern Israel & Judah, and the Post-Exilic restoration. (3) The *bottom level* includes all the individual narratives that make up the preceding levels. The authors cogently point out:

> ...every individual Old Testament narrative (the bottom level) is at least a part of the greater narrative of Israel's history in the world (the middle level), which in turn is a part of the ultimate narrative of God's creation and his redemption of it (the top level). This ultimate narrative goes beyond the Old Testament through the New Testament. You will not fully do justice to any individual narrative without recognizing its part within the other two (Fee and Stuart 1993:80).

The unified nature of the Storybook does not cease with the Old Testament. Witherington (1994) argues persuasively that Pauline theology cannot be understood properly without first comprehending all the stories that inform it previously. These stories would include the Christian community story (including Paul's story), the Christ story (central), Israel's story, and a world gone astray (Abraham's and Adam's stories). Paul's linear preaching and teaching found their context in the unified story of the sacred Storybook.

Swartley (1994) continues the thesis that previous biblical stories inform latter stories when he claims that Israel's Scriptural traditions shape the content and structure of the Synoptic Gospels. He argues that four streams of Israel's tradition can be observed: (1) exodus-Sinai (salvation through the perfect works and wonders of Jesus Christ), (2) way-contest (victorious discipleship focused on the Promised Land, driven by self-denial and servanthood), (3) temple (God judges inappropriate behavior, worshipped by all peoples, not a select few), and (4) kingship (a rejected King destroys all opposing powers by rising from the dead, and reigns so that others can join his kingdom). The stories read and taught in the synagogues and homes shaped the Synoptic narratives.

The New Testament builds upon the Old Testament, rather than merely adds to it. The four Gospels find their roots embedded deeply in the Old Testament. The Epistles find their framework in Acts, a natural outgrowth of the Gospels. Revelation builds on everything that precedes it, bringing a unified finality to all. McClendon argues correctly:

> The life of Christ cannot be told without the whole New Testament, without the whole history of the "God Movement," without the whole human story *annis domini*—in the years of

the Lord. In this sense, the lives of our saints significantly participate in the life of Christ; telling their stories is a part of telling *that* story (1974:201).

God's Sacred Storybook

⇑⇑

Adam & Eve's Story

⇑⇑

Abraham's Story

⇑⇑

Israel's Story

⇑⇑

Jesus Christ's Story

⇑ ⇑

Christian Community's Story

Figure 2. God's unified sacred Storybook

And the whole New Testament stands upon the Old Testament. The Jeweler has set the individual diamonds into a finished product—an eye-catching tennis bracelet.

Discerns God's Theological Categories

The unified Storybook respects the past. It recognizes that God has entered human history with an agenda for all creation: to establish his Kingdom. It recognizes that this agenda includes certain absolutes (theological categories), divinely appropriate for all generations and ethnicities. The past helps guarantee the preservation of God's sacred Story in the present.

The unified Storybook respects the present. In a nonthreatening way, the sacred Storybook invites people to reflect upon the individual stories (bottom level) found within its pages, in hopes that the audience will eventually discern God's redemptive story (top level). Before reaching the top level, other stories from the bottom and middle levels will provide background textual information and address felt needs. In that God's agenda addresses the total person, such needs must be respected, even when it is considered foreign from one's own perspective. Yet, to stop short of the top level is to deny the theological category that unifies the Storybook, Jesus Christ.

By recognizing the theological category that unifies the Storybook, it then becomes possible to sift all surrounding theological categories identified by anyone— whether Westerners, Asians, Native Americans, Latinos, Indians, Africans, feminists—through this grid. While the theologies may be different or even contradictory, as noted above, no true individual theology will contradict or challenge the life and work of Jesus Christ. Rather, they will elevate Jesus Christ to his rightful Kingly role. Just as a maze puzzle is much easier to put together after a visual overview of the finished product, so the same is true for discerning God's theological categories in the Storybook.

As an aggregate, diverse theologies have the potential to expand all peoples' worldviews in relation to their concept of God. Theologies missed by one people group, due to cultural blinders, can now be augmented thanks to the insights of others. Diverse theologies offer the community of faith an opportunity for spiritual growth.

Diverse theologies should also have opportunity for challenge. In that theologies are socially constructed, all require reconstruction over time.[1] Open dialogue allows this to happen. Such interaction should prove mutually corrective as theological patterns emerge (or fail to do so) throughout the sacred Storybook. Creators and advocates of the various theologies must demonstrate humility so that personal-communal preferences become subservient to the sacred Storybook of the King of Kings. Those from competing viewpoints must also fight their bias for holism or fragmentation. Both styles will be necessary to meet the different personal/collective expectations, and expand them. Preference for either perspective should not deter acceptance of valid theologies coming from those of different persuasion. Such attitudes will help make it possible for all peoples to discover God's repertoire of theological categories.

Respects Literary Genres

Recognizing that the Storybook contains numerous literary genres, and utilizing the appropriate exegetical tools will go a long way in identifying God's theological categories. Proof texting will be challenged, as will the perception that God is interested primarily in abstract, propositional statements. A more balanced picture of characters will appear. For example, 1 and 2 Samuel provide the historical facts of the life of David. The Psalms add the affective domain, providing inside glimpses into David's anxiety, anguish, agitation, praise and faith. By combining the two accounts, a more human David emerges. To do this, however, the three books require different exegetical tools.

Respect for the various literary styles of the Storybook in Bible study receives greater emphasis today than in the past. Authors such as Gordon Fee and Douglas Stuart, Leland Ryken, and Kenneth Bailey have provided excellent studies on this topic. Exegetical helps for translators have advanced beyond the interpretation of phrases and words to the analysis of entire letters and books as genuine pieces of literature. These advances will help thrust people beyond the individual narratives to the story of redemption and farther. While the Storybook is definitely broader than literature, as literature it must be treated as such.

Unites Evangelism to Follow-up

Unlike many Christian workers, the Storybook refuses to divorce evangelism from follow-up. Because a unified story exists, potential disciples must be alerted to the big picture. They must become knowledgeable about the protagonist and antagonist, the key players, the plot, and the challenges and costs the story will bring individually and collectively. Only then can they interact intelligently with God's sacred Story. More time spent in front-loading the gospel message with case studies about God's interaction with his creation (see Fee and Stuart's three levels) should result in a clearer grasp of the message, along with the expected commitment level of those who become followers, joyful obedience.

The sacred Storybook does not conclude that people simply change faith allegiances; it calls them to establish God's Kingdom. This Kingdom will require a certain type of individual/community. Building on the foundation of the gospel message, Christian workers must remind the young disciples that God promises to be there for them during floods, Red Sea crossings, pilgrimages, leadership changes, the construction of tabernacles, encounters with the deceased, the presence of hostile evil spirits, persecution, dreams, inclement weather, sickness, disputes, sin, and yes—even death. Their beliefs and behavior will play a major role in the expansion of God's Kingdom. Knowing the big picture will help them interpret the inevitable challenges of daily life (snapshots) from God's global perspective.

Conclusion

The Bible is not just a collection of isolated stories; it is God's unified Storybook. While each of the 66 documents that comprise the sacred Storybook has its own beauty and value, the eloquence of each is maximized when taken as a collective whole. Just as the aggregate value of the diamonds in a tennis bracelet far outweighs the value of a single diamond, so the value of this Storybook far outweighs the value of its individual documents.

The next chapter will consider the Storyline that unifies the sacred Storybook: the story of Jesus Christ.

[1] Robert Saucy's *The Case for Progressive Dispensationalism* serves as an excellent case-in-point on the issue of review of theologies.

Reflection:

What new questions does this chapter raise for you?

In what ways have you promoted a fragmented Storybook?

What ministry changes do you anticipate making?

For Further Reading:

Barr, David L.
    1987   New Testament Story: An Introduction. Belmont, CA:
            Wadsworth Publishers.
Childs, B. S.
    1993   Biblical Theology of the Old and New Testaments:
            Theological Reflections on the Christian Bible. Minneapolis:
            Augsburg/Fortress.
Pratt, Richard L., Jr.
    1990   He Gave Us Stories: The Bible Student's Guide to
            Interpreting Old Testament Narratives. Brentwood, TN:
            Wolgemuth & Hyatt, Publishers, Inc.
Ryken, Leland
    1984   How to Read the Bible as Literature. Grand Rapids, MI:
            Academie Books.
Ryken, Leland and Tremper Longman, III, eds.
    1993   A Complete Literary Guide to the Bible. Grand Rapids, MI:
            Zondervan Publishing House.
Swartley, Willard M.
    1994   Israel's Scripture Traditions and the Synoptic Gospels.
            Peabody, MA: Hendrickson Publishers, Inc.
Witherington, III, Ben
    1994   Paul's Narrative Thought World: The Tapestry of Tragedy
            and Triumph. Louisville, KY: Westminster/John Knox
            Press.

4
The Storyline

Christ is not only the Center of Scripture;
He is also the circumference of Scripture.
Belatedly, but surely, more and more of us are
rediscovering the significance of these twin truths.
DAVID HESSELGRAVE

The Storybook exists to tell the
Story....As you struggle to get the story out,
you are driven back to getting the story straight.
GABRIEL FACKRE

The sacred Storybook begins to make sense once the Storyline is made clear. This chapter attempts to identify the Storyline, look for ways to guard it over generations and ethnic diversity (2 Tim. 1:14), and suggest paradigm shifts (changes in the fundamental ways things normally get done) that may be necessary for the first two objectives to become a ministry reality.

Identify the Storyline

The sacred Storybook is an extensive piece of literature comprised of 66 individual books and letters. Eventually, believers divided the 66 books into two major scenes, the Old Testament and the New Testament. Even so divided, the two Testaments remain intricately interlinked as one story.

One of the books in the New Testament, The Gospel According to John, provides some clues that link the Storyline through the Testaments. John begins to articulate the story of God by pointing immediately to the Storyline. In broad strokes, John paints a picture of Creation, Jesus' role in the Creation, the possibility for all people to recognize him, Jesus' ability to perform sign-miracles, advocates who propagate the Christ-centered message, and followers who participate in certain rituals and requirements that distinguish them from other community groups. For John, the Storyline is the message of God's reign initiated and instituted by the sinless Savior. Jesus Christ is the Storyline of God's sacred Storybook.

Jesus also clarifies who the Storyline is by pointing out what the Old Testament writers prophesied many years prior to his birth. While talking to two despondent disciples headed for Emmaus, Jesus admonishes them for their lack of faith and fortitude. "'How foolish you are, and how slow of heart to believe all that the prophets have spoken! Did not the Christ have to suffer these things and then enter his glory?' And beginning with Moses and all the Prophets, he explained to them what was said in all the Scriptures concerning himself" (Lk. 24:25-27).

Since no complete record of Jesus' discourse exists, one can only speculate as to what Jesus may have included that caused the disciples' hearts to burn within them. He may have discussed how Moses and the prophets prophesied that the Storyline of the sacred Storybook would be born in Bethlehem, born of a virgin, taken to Egypt, preceded by a forerunner, betrayed by a friend for thirty pieces of silver, slapped, spit upon, mocked, and insulted.

Jesus may have referred to specific events, such as when the soldiers gambled for the Storyline's clothes, nailed him to a cross as a perfect sacrifice, or the results of the resurrection: the destruction of the power of Satan and death and the forgiveness of sin. He may have highlighted how the Storyline became a Prophet greater than Moses, a Priest like Melchizedek, and a King like David who will reign forever over a new heaven and earth.

Jesus could have included other analogies from the sacred Storybook to help the disciples recognize the Storyline: the perfected Adam, the single door of the ark and the tabernacle (mediator) that led to safety and God's presence, the sheep without blemish or broken bones offered during the Passover, the cloud and fire that led the Israelites in the desert, the water that God graciously provided for those dying of thirst in the desert, the daily manna that God sent down from heaven as promised, the brazen snake that Moses hung on a pole that provided healing for all who obeyed, the scapegoat released in the desert to carry away the sins of Israel, the Good Shepherd, the cities of refuge, the wise counselor like Solomon, the bright and morning star, the lily of the valley, the revived Jonah, the lion of Judah, the Alpha and the Omega.

Whoever the key characters, or whatever the key events, prophecies and/or analogies Jesus may have discussed with the disciples during the journey to Emmaus, they became convinced beyond a shadow of a doubt that he was the Storyline of the sacred Storybook (See Figure 3).

The cloudy memory of despondent disciples, then, now, or in the future will never negate Jesus' preeminent role as the Storyline (Heb. 13:8).

Guard the Storyline

Dedicated Christian workers attempt to communicate the Storyline of the sacred Storybook in word and deed so that listeners value, accept, and practice it, just as faithful followers of Christ did before and after Saul's trip to Damascus. To help ensure that this goal will become a reality, Christian workers should answer a series of often overlooked questions that address the unbeliever (who we will call the mariner), the message, the messenger, and the mode of communication (see Figure 4). Guarding the Storyline begins by asking and answering the right questions.

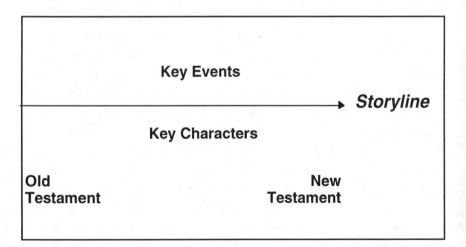

Figure 3. Identifying the Storyline

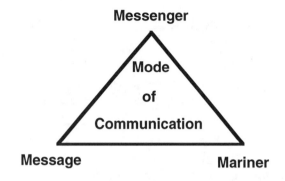

Figure 4. Asking the right questions

Ask the Right Questions about the Mariner

In sailing the seas of life, the unbelieving mariner seeks to chart a course in life that will reach a safe spiritual harbor. In that the life-experiences of each mariner differs considerably because each port of call differs, so do their worldviews and expectations about life.

Christian workers often overlook the fact that different worldviews and expectations should call for different ministry approaches. Rather than take time to create new evangelism models, they often rely on models that won them to Christ or those used by esteemed mentors. For example, the Four Spiritual Laws, or some form of it, can be found in use around the world. But in what ports of call will this model prove most effective? Should Christian workers assume that this model will sail smoothly into any port? Tom Houston challenges this assumption:

> In Russia, people were used to the Communist Party telling them how great and wonderful the worker's republic is. They were used to glowing, optimistic lies. So when an evangelist goes in with stories about how great and wonderful the kingdom of God is, and tells them glowing, optimistic testimonies, do you know what they say? "We thought Christians were different" (1993:258).

A Christian worker who recently returned from ministry in the former U.S.S.R. concurs when he made this observation in one of my classes:

> The four laws did not relate to many of the problems that they were going through with government, family, society, and the political, economic unrest. Also, the four laws assumes that they already believed in God. This was not the case since many of them had been taught all of their lives that God did not exist.

Because a mariner's expectations vary, so must evangelism methodologies. This leads to the first question: *Who is the mariner?* By identifying the mariner's worldview, Christian workers will receive valuable insights as to how to navigate the port of call in which they wish to communicate the Storyline.

A second question that could be asked is: *What type of decision-making pattern does the mariner prefer?* While Western evangelism models often call for individual decisions for Christ, the New Testament is replete with family or group decisions (Jn. 1:40-42, 4:53; Acts 9:35; 14:1,19-20; 16:15,30; 18:8). Does the mariner prefer to make individual decisions? Peer decisions? Nuclear family decisions? Extended family decisions? Community decisions? Which type of decision-making preference demands more time? Does the mariner respond more readily to questions that focus on guilt or shame? How the contact culture makes decisions should have tremendous impact on evangelism approaches.

Another question that could be asked is: *What will it cost the mariner to become a believer?* Will a positive response to the Storyline result in certain social costs? family costs? economic costs? political costs? The answer(s) to this question will alert the Christian workers to the mariner's deep-seated concerns, felt needs and the price tags associated with each. Evangelism methodologies should be adjusted accordingly.

Ask the Right Questions about the Message

The Apostle Paul, a recipient of significant supernatural insights into the Storyline, summarized the message in 1 Corinthians 15:

> For what I received I passed on to you as of first importance: that Christ died for our sins according to the Scriptures, that he was buried, that he was resurrected on the third day according to the Scriptures, and that he appeared to Peter, and then to the Twelve. After that, he appeared to more than five hundred... (15:3-6).

The simply stated Storyline found in the above passage carries weighty implicit information. Those who communicate the Storyline would do well do ask the following question: *What are the basic components that comprise the gospel message?*

Ryken offers Christian workers a way to plumb the depth and extent of the Storyline when he suggests that "Stories are always built out of three basic ingredients: settings, characters, and plot (action)" (1984:35). In relation to the Storyline found in the 1 Corinthians passage of the sacred Storybook, the visible setting would include the Mediterranean and adjacent areas, while the invisible setting would include the heavens, earth, and hell. As for characters, the protagonist would be the Trinity, supported by an entourage of benevolent angels while the antagonist would be Satan, supported by legions of malevolent angels. The plot reveals an ongoing spiritual battle between the forces of good and evil as they vie for the allegiance of God's people, separated from him because of sin and unbelief. However, the battle has a predetermined conclusion: Jesus Christ will establish his kingdom reign and provide an abode of comfort for his faithful followers; while Satan and his cohorts (those who fail to believe/obey the Storyline) will eventually be cast into the eternal lake of fire.

More key components of the Storyline could be included, such as personal and collective sin, personal and cosmic judgment, the human soul and spirit, substitution, resurrection, grace and works, repentance, personal and collective faith, and transformed morals. It should be obvious that the brief message stated in 1 Corinthians is much more complex than meets the eye.

This observation indicates the need to ask a further question: *What does the mariner understand about the basic components of the Storyline?* A simple way to find the answer to this question would be for the messengers to list all components of the Storyline they can identify. Then, in a separate column, note the mariner's understanding of each component. Communication bridges, barriers, and gaps should become apparent through such a study.

When the messengers complete this comparative exercise, they will be ready for the next question: *How much front-loading of the gospel message will the mariner require?* Front-loading the gospel means providing the mariner with all necessary foundational components (characters and events) of the Storyline in order to neutralize any gaps or barriers that may exist. For example, traditional Ifugao believe God *(Meknengan)* is distant from them, and any malicious acts an Ifugao commits toward another Ifugao have virtually no impact on his or her relationship to God. For the Ifugao, the consequences of sin between people flow vertically, not horizontally. They do not believe that their separation from God stems from personal or collective sin. In fact, should they sin, the Ifugao would construe that God caused them to commit it.

For Jesus' role as Restorer of broken relationships with God to make sense to the Ifugao, I had to spend significant time allowing Scripture stories to challenge and correct deeply held erroneous beliefs about God. Presenting the brief message of 1 Corinthians 15 or the Four Spiritual Laws initially could have resulted in great distortion or delusion of the Storyline. This leads to the next question: *How should evangelism connect to follow-up?*

Presenting foundational background information for the Storyline takes time. But it does more than provide time for reflection about cultural gaps or barriers to the Storyline, as in the case of the Ifugao. The additional Old and New Testament stories of characters and events also lay an excellent foundation to build upon once the mariner decides to drop anchor in the Storyline's harbor. The stories introduce (in sequence when possible) key characters of various cultures and the doctrines they communicate, such as the Trinity, Satan, creation, God's reign, justice, sin, law, judgment, grace, prophecies of a coming Savior, covenants between God and man, repentance, justification by faith, all in a human context. This approach moves beyond communicating the need to believe in Jesus to God's definition of believing, which calls for a lifelong journey; it moves beyond a New Testament, middle-of-the-book presentation of the Storyline, to incorporate the big picture of the sacred Storybook.

Christian workers who communicate case studies about God's interaction with his creation will provide mariners with a broad understanding of the Storyline, as well as the commitment expectations for those embarking on the Christian-life voyage: joyful obedience. Spending significant time in front-loading the Storyline will not only help guard the gospel, it will also provide a solid foundation for ongoing follow-up. Like Paul Harvey, these messengers are not content until they narrate the "Rest of the Story."

Ask the Right Questions about the Messenger

Not only must the Christian worker ask, *Who is the mariner?;* he or she must also ask an equally important question: *Who is the messenger?* Just as the mariner reflects a particular worldview and life expectations, so does the messenger.

Hiebert defines ethnocentrism as: "...the tendency of people to judge other cultures by the values and assumptions of their own culture. Of course, by one's own culture's criteria, all other cultures appear inferior" (1976:38). Ethnocentrism influences the way the messenger views others, interprets the Storybook, and selects evangelism models. To avoid ethnocentric biases in any area, the messenger should become cognizant of the values that drive his or her worldview. A values test can help accomplish this (see Lingenfelter and Mayers 1986:30-33).

Peter, like every effective cross-cultural messenger, had to experience several cultural conversions. After three years with Jesus, hearing the Great Commission, being present at Pentecost, it took voices, visions, angels, and the Holy Spirit to get him to enter the house of Cornelius. After this leap of faith Peter acknowledged: "God showed me that I should not call any man common or unclean...I now realize how true it is that God does not show favoritism but accepts men from every nation who fear him and do what is right" (Acts 10:34-35).

Removing layers of ethnocentrism is like peeling an onion. There are numerous layers to peel off, and it can be a tearful experience. Peter experienced another layer of onion peeling when he tasted Paul's wrath for refusing to eat with Gentiles once the Jews arrived (Gal. 2).

Most of the popular evangelistic models used today cannot be found in the evangelism case studies in Acts. One looks in vain for Peter or Paul using the "Four Spiritual Laws," "Evangelism Explosion," "First Steps to God," or "Chronological Teaching." The absence of invitationalism as practiced today also stands out. Examples of raising a hand, walking an aisle (introduced by Charles G. Finney in the nineteenth century), or signing a card are conspicuously absent. Because worldview influences the model selection made by the messenger, it would be good to ask: *What assumptions/values drive the evangelistic tools/models selected?*

The absence of such models in Scripture should alert messengers to the fact that behind all evangelistic models stand human agents influenced by corporate and individual worldviews. For example, the "Four Spiritual Laws" model requires listeners to assume that God exists, life is orderly and planned, individuals make decisions, and the number "four" is positive. While such assumptions and values create harbors for some mariners, they become sandbars for others. To illustrate, while the number "four" signifies wholeness (the circle of life) for the Native Americans, it signals death for some Asians. When messengers fail to investigate the assumptions and values of their evangelism models, or contextualize them for specific audiences, they can easily confuse the Storyline for the mariner.

Ask the Right Questions about the Mode of Communication

Messengers communicating cross-culturally often use modes of communication familiar and comfortable to them. This preference may make the Bible one of the most poorly taught books in the world. To avoid the assumption that one communication mode works well in any mariner's port of entry, the messenger would do well to ask: *What delivery system does the mariner prefer (so the message is comprehensible and reproducible)?* Does the mariner prefer to chart a course after consulting a broad map of the area? Must the big idea precede smaller ideas? How important is chronology? Analogies? Binary pairs? How does the mariner analyze ideas? Synthesize ideas? Does the mariner prefer communicating abstractly or concretely? By a series of analogies that relate to one another around a central idea (chiasmus)? How does the mariner use questions? Does the mariner have a number breakdown preference for oral or written communication, such as "threes" (three blind mice) or "fours" (circle of life)? Should lesson application focus on the individual? Corporate group? Because delivery systems vary from port to port, wise messengers will attempt to identify and utilize them.

Analyzing the mariner's response to the mode of communication and message leads to the next question: *How will the messenger know if the mode of communication influenced the mariner to drop anchor in Jesus' harbor?* While no human being can discern the spiritual status of another, it is possible to conduct some analysis to ascertain a mariner's comprehension of the Storyline. In *Passing the Baton* (Steffen 1993b), I identified several areas that messengers can investigate to accomplish this. As a new professing believer testifies to others about his or her faith, listen for the concept that Jesus Christ has become the lone substitute to restore a broken relationship with God. Look for: (1) a desire to learn about the Storybook, (2) cultural-specific evidence that demonstrates a switch in faith-allegiance (repentance), and (3) a reordering of moral values and material assets. Listen for comments from close friends. If Christianity has taken root, their friends will be some of the first to notice. These, and other criteria, will help messengers assess the mariner's true comprehension of the Storyline as well as ability to communicate it effectively to others.

Evangelism Paradigm Shifts

Changing old habits requires a paradigm shift. Implementing the findings to the above oft-overlooked questions may require the messenger to make a number of paradigm shifts when communicating the Storyline to searching mariners (see Table 2). The same may be true for messengers evangelizing those with different learning styles, different genders or generations, or ethnics in the work force, on university campuses, or in the neighborhood.

One of these paradigm shifts may call for the messenger to move beyond the presentation of isolated pictures to the big picture. Just as Paul tied the Storyline to the Old and New Testaments (Rom. 1:1-2; 1 Cor. 15:1-6), so messengers should attempt to communicate a message that spans both Testaments. Such an overview can address existing cultural bridges, barriers, and knowledge gaps. A diachronic overview of the redemptive Storyline will help avoid the fragmentation present in many evangelism models today, provide sufficient time for the mariner to sort out the truth, all the while laying a solid foundation for ongoing follow-up.

A second paradigm shift that may be required is the move beyond words to deeds. Evangelism models often emphasize believing an idea rather than demonstrating transformed behavior. When a mariner drops the anchor of faith in Jesus' harbor, the demand for a change in lifestyle should come as no surprise. Patterson & Scoggins correctly point out: "If we merely help converts to 'decide' to 'accept' Jesus—a concept foreign to the New Testament—we will have few committed disciples" (1993:25).

Luke demonstrates the connection between word and deed: "When the people heard this, they were cut to the heart and said to Peter and the other apostles, 'Brothers, what shall we do?'" (Acts 2:37). Later, he documents Saul's response: "Who are you, Lord?...What shall I do, Lord?" (Acts 22:8,10). Foundational evangelism case studies from both Testaments will help the mariner tie walk to talk.

Another possible paradigm shift may call for a move beyond meeting the mariner's felt needs to addressing his or her supracultural need, i.e. the need to restore a broken relationship with God through the substitutionary work of Jesus Christ. All too often, messengers communicate the Storyline through word and deed in a way that meets felt needs, but fails to address the mariner's supracultural need. Arias rightly takes exception to this unbalanced practice:

Table 2

Paradigm Shifts in Evangelism

Isolated pictures	⇨	Big picture
Word	⇨	Deed
Felt needs	⇨	Supracultural need
Quick formulas	⇨	Character studies
Arguments	⇨	Narrative
Salesperson	⇨	Storyteller

> We need to correct the almost-invincible tendency of our
> evangelization to present the gospel in terms of "blessings"—
> benefits to be received, answers to all our questions, remedy
> to all our evils, new life to be enjoyed, a future state to be
> secured—without at the same time presenting the challenges,
> demands, and tasks of the kingdom (1984:105-106).

To assure that costly grace does not become replaced
by cheap grace, the messenger must announce cleanly a
credible conflict (Brueggemann 1993). Challenge must
accompany comfort in the messenger's presentation of the
Storyline, no matter what the mariner's cultural costs.

Moving beyond quick formulas to character studies
may be a fourth paradigm shift required. Not everyone is
impressed with getting to the bottom line as fast as

possible. Relational oriented people prefer strong relationships any day over impersonal, quick formulas. This includes a relationship with the messenger. And it moves beyond the messenger to the content of the message. Relational oriented people relate well to character studies for it is in these stories that they find themselves and their people. For the audience that does not appreciate quick formulas, messengers will do well to package the message in concrete characters.

A fifth paradigm shift that may be necessary calls for a move beyond argument to narrative. Many evangelism models present the Storyline as a set of systematized ideas ready to be argued. Proponents have thought through the anticipated objections, marshaled supporting data, and developed a logical rebuttal. In many cases, however, such polemic debates only serve to cement the convictions and philosophical beliefs of those from both camps. Right answers do not necessarily guarantee acceptance. Eisenhower's remarks ring true:

> The apologists...are bold in championing the faith, and defiant in opposing the culture. Yet something is missing so that for all their wisdom, for all their marshaling of evidence, and for all their aggressive argumentation—the whole effort at defending Christianity just seems too...defensive (1995:6).

Eisenhower goes on to argue that a "fatal flaw" in apologetics is the ignoring of narrative. For the audience that does not appreciate polemics, or does, wise messengers will frame their core ideas in narratives.

A friend of mine evangelizing Arabs in Lebanon began with Josh McDowell's *Evidence That Demands A Verdict* and C.S. Lewis' *Mere Christianity*. The Arabs, however, would not agree with the rationalized apologetics that Jesus was either a liar or a lunatic. "I never got anywhere," he told me, "the Arabs are storytellers!" Just as the Storyline became flesh and blood, so must the message. For many people, human case studies from the Bible or personal testimonies will prove more powerful than the greatest logic presented systematically.

Another possible paradigm shift closely related to the fifth may require a messenger to move beyond selling (salesperson) to telling (storyteller). Rather than seeing the Storyline as a product to sell, the messenger envisions it as a Story to be told.

The mariner can take at least two approaches to communicate "The Greatest Story Ever Told." The first calls for a journey through Scripture, accenting personal and collective stories that define the Storyline (Lk. 24; Acts 7). The second calls for telling one's faithstory (Chapter 5). As Fackre has so eloquently noted: "Evangelism connects the story with my story" (1975:59). Telling one's faithstory is not a product to be sold, but an invitation to join in a journey.

Conclusion

Has any good Story come out of Nazareth? The answer is a resounding "Yes!" The story is recorded in the sacred Storybook, and it is the responsibility of the messengers not only to identify it, but to preserve it. Jesus Christ is the Storyline of the sacred Storybook.

Wise messengers will move beyond identification and protection of the Storyline; they will also attempt to communicate it in a way that makes it easy for the mariner not only to grasp, but also to accurately pass on to family and friends. This may require the messenger to make a number of difficult paradigm shifts. This may also require an in-depth investigation of the storyteller's cultural landscape.

Once the messenger completes the above tasks, it is time to tell the tale; it is time to become a storyteller.

Reflection:

What new questions does this chapter raise for you in relation to evangelism-discipleship?

What other paradigm shifts may be necessary?

What ministry changes do you anticipate making?

For Further Reading:

Baxter, J. Sidlow
   1966   Explore the Book: A Basic and Broadly Interpretive Course
          of Bible Study From Genesis to Revelation. Grand Rapids,
          MI: Zondervan Publishing House.
Brueggemann, Walter
   1993   Biblical Perspectives on Evangelism: Living in a Three-
          Storied Universe. Nashville, TN: Abington Press.
Dyrness, William A.
   1983   Let the Earth Rejoice! A Biblical Theology of Holistic
          Mission. Westchester, IL: Crossway Books.
McIlwain, Trevor
   1987   Building on Firm Foundations: Guidelines for Evangelism
          and Teaching Believers, Vol. 1. Sanford, FL: New Tribes
          Mission.
Steffen, Tom A.
   1993a   Don't Show the Jesus Film... Evangelical Missions
           Quarterly, 29(3): 272-275.

5
The Storyteller

Tell the next generation that God is here. Ps 48:14, JB

That man was a great story teller. I once
asked him where he got those stories. That is
when he told me about the Book. That is what he
called it. The Book. That was my first Christian
book. The Bible. Yes, he gave it to me. It was the most
colorful book I had ever seen. I read the O.T. up to Acts
within a year...Oh, I miss that man. I know he will be
surprised to hear my life story when I see him in Heaven.
CLEMENT MUWELE

Many messengers in the United States find
witnessing to others about Jesus Christ very difficult.
Barna's survey concludes:

During the course of the year, barely one-third of all adults
make an effort to share their religious faith with others who
possess other beliefs. Should they evangelize, they generally

emerge from their evangelistic adventure not with a feeling of
joy, obedience, impact, hope or gratitude, but with a feeling
of defeat (1993:47).

Whether Barna's data details same culture to same culture
witnessing, or crosscultural witnessing, is not clear. It is
clear, however, that most messengers find witnessing
extremely uncomfortable. Is there some way messengers
can gain confidence to witness to people of like cultural
background, especially for the majority without the gift of
evangelism? To people of different cultural backgrounds?
In this chapter, I will explore three modes of evangelism-
discipleship: recital of ideas and images, recital of events
and characters, and recital of personal faithstories.
Particular emphasis is given to the smithing of stories,
including faithstories (personal testimonies), as a possible
tool to communicate the Storyline with confidence and
power.

An Original Storytelling Tradition

Boomershine cogently points out the evolution of the
meaning of the term "gospel." He notes that the term
"gospel" is a shortened form of an Old English word,
"godspell," which means "good tale." The best Latin
equivalent, *evangelium,* meant "a tale whose telling had
power" (1988:16). Later on, the term "gospel" became
associated with the four Gospels: Matthew, Mark, Luke,
and John. Still later, the term incorporated the summation
of the basic, abstract beliefs of Christianity. Boomershine
concludes:

> The Church now tends to think of the gospel as a set of
> abstract ideas based on the study of the canonical documents
> but divorced from story. The gospel has lost its original

character as a living storytelling tradition of messengers who told the good news of the victory of Jesus (1991:17).

Boomershine stands in good company when he argues that "the gospel was originally a storytelling tradition" (1988:16). Niebuhr concurs:

> The preaching of the early Christian church was not an argument for the existence of God nor an admonition to follow the dictates of some common human conscience, unhistorical and super-social in character. It was primarily a simple recital of the great events connected with the historical appearance of Jesus Christ and a confession of what had happened to the community of disciples (Niebuhr in Hauerwas and Jones 1989:21).

John, writing in the first century, cannot overlook the importance of personal testimony in drawing others to Christ:

> That which was from the beginning, which we have heard, which we have seen with our eyes, which we have looked at and our hands have touched—this we proclaim concerning the Word of life...so that you also may have fellowship with us (1 Jn. 1:1-3).

Could the recital of the great events of the sacred Storybook return messengers of the Storyline to something neglected over time, narrative evangelism-discipleship? Could the same be true for personal faithstories? Could narrative evangelism-discipleship produce a host of bold, confident messengers who can provide direction from the sacred Storybook to lost mariners sailing the turbulent seas of life?

While numerous ways exist to communicate the Storyline through narrative evangelism, this chapter will examine three which move generally from the abstract mode of communication to the concrete, from the apologetic to dialogue.

Recital of Ideas and Images

One way that messengers can narrate the Storyline is the recital of key ideas and images that conceptualize Christianity (see Figure 5). When Jesus met clandestinely with Nicodemus he used images of childbirth and the snake in the desert to convey what it means to become a legitimate member of the Kingdom of God (Jn. 3).

When the Ethiopian found it difficult to understand the meaning behind an innocent lamb slaughtered, Philip "began with that very passage of scripture and told him the good news about Jesus" (Acts 8:35). As the fog dissipated, the mariner discovered the Storyline in the image of a sacrificial lamb.

Paul seems to have taken a more abstract approach than Philip when witnessing to Felix and Drusilla:

> Several days later Felix came with his wife Drusilla, who was a Jewess. He sent for Paul and listened to him as he spoke about faith in Christ Jesus. As Paul discoursed on righteousness, self-control and the judgment to come, Felix was afraid and said, "That's enough for now!" (Acts 24:24-25).

It is not stated whether Paul wrapped the abstract ideas of righteousness, self-control, and the judgment in concrete forms. However, Luke notes that Paul's message began to hit home with Felix and Drusilla. A frightened Felix conveniently cut off the challenging concepts.

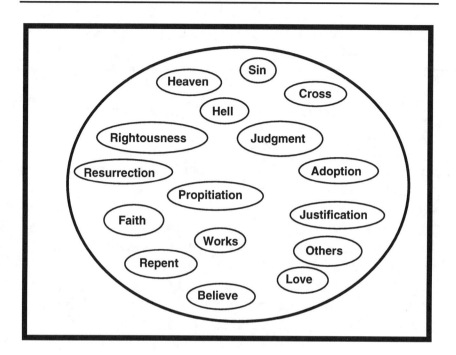

Figure 5. Storyline as abstract ideas and images

Communicating the Storyline through abstract ideas requires a certain mindset. Communicators who prefer this learning style tend to enjoy reflecting on and responding to ideas. Not all messengers or mariners, howevwe, will feel comfortable with this mode of communication. Rather, they may prefer one that ties together "reason and imagination, fact and mystery" (Ryken 1987:39), such as the teaching images used by Jesus and Philip. This move beyond the recital of abstract concepts to concrete images can help drive home a messenger's key points. But communicators of the Storyline can take another powerful concrete approach, the recital of Bible stories.

Recital of Events and Characters

The names of the traders who told the residents of Jericho stories about God's interactions with the Israelites did not find a place in Scripture. Nor can readers be sure they had a relationship with God. Nevertheless, Rahab came to know about the true God through the intriguing stories of these traders: "We have heard how the Lord dried up the water..." (Josh. 2:10-11).

New Testament readers can find numerous examples of Christian messengers who recited stories of biblical events and characters when communicating the Storyline (see Figure 6). Stephen's recital of the great events of Israel's history did not receive as positive a response initially as did Philip's (Acts 7). Within a short time, Stephen's listeners reacted against the piercing truth humanized through the events and characters storied; they stoned the storyteller to death.

But Stephen's stories did not go unheeded by all present. The young man caring for the robes of those casting the deadly stones would find it hard to forget the powerful images etched in his mind through Stephen's stories. Just as the stones hit their fleshly mark, resulting in physical death of the storyteller, so the stories hit the spiritual heart of Saul, challenging him to reconsider the Christ story. The great events of the covenant given to Abraham, Joseph's captivity in Egypt, the life of Moses, and the switch from the tabernacle to the temple transformed Saul the persecutor of "the way" to Paul the persuader of "the way."

An example of Paul the persuader can be found when he witnessed to the "men of Athens." Paul told his audience about creation, the placement of nations, the closeness of God to them, what God expected from his human creation, and the consequences of challenging the Creator-God. The audience was split; some believed while others sneered (Acts 17:22-34).

Hearing about God at work in the lives of people and events often challenges listeners in a nonthreatening way to reflect upon what role God should rightfully play in their

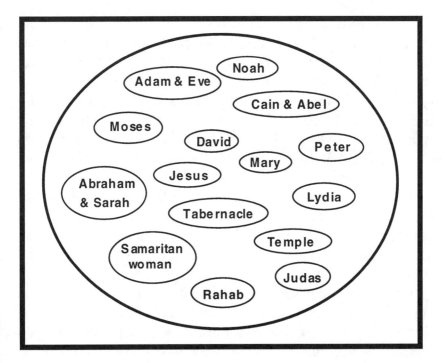

Figure 6. Storyline as events and characters

lives. The historical times, geographic locations, or cultural differences tend to take a back seat as the hearer's own story resonates through the lives of the characters and events storied. Such earthy stories cause faith, reason, and imagination to converge. The recital of the characters and events points to and helps clarify the Jesus story.

If the storying of distant events and characters is so powerful, will not the recital of contemporary faithstories carry similar power?

Recital of Faithstories

Listeners find people's faithstories contagious, challenging, and convicting. After perceiving that Jesus was the Storyline of the Storybook, the Samaritan woman returned to her hometown of Sychar to tell her friends what happened. John tells us what transpired: "Many of the Samaritans from that town believed because of the woman's testimony" (Jn. 4:39). The faithstory of a forgiven prostitute infected her neighbors, resulting in numerous new faithstories.

Sight restored in a blind man brought challenge to the Pharisees. They wanted to know how a sinner could cause a blind man to see. The healed man testified that the alleged "sinner" was a prophet (Jn. 9:17). Not satisfied, the Pharisees questioned the healed man's parents before questioning the man again. The healed man responded candidly: "Whether he is a sinner or not, I don't know. One thing I do know, I was blind but now I see....Why do you want to hear it again? Do you want to become his disciples, too" (Jn. 9:25,27)? Stunned and threatened, the Pharisees hurled insults at the confident healed man.

Paul often drew upon his faithstory to defend himself or his Christian faith (see Figure 7). Listeners heard about his birthplace (Tarsus), his Roman citizenship by birth, his education under the renowned Gamaliel, his former religious beliefs, practices, and passion, his intense persecution of Christians, his blindness, his meeting Christ on the road to Damascus, his restored sight, his zealous witness for Christ, and so forth. Paul often provided listeners an overview of his life, recounting his past and present activities, along with his future expectations.

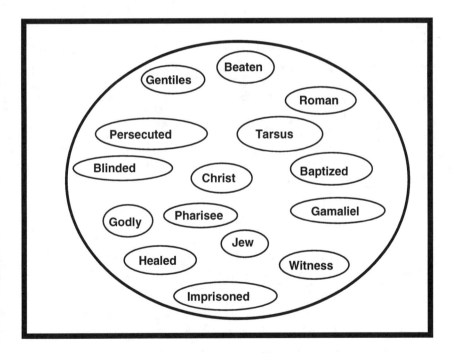

Figure 7. Storyline as personal faithstories

The recital of personal faithstories may take place in a host of settings. This powerful communication tool, however, does not guarantee the conversion of its listeners. Even so, the Samaritan woman case study demonstrates a possible positive result. Whether listeners are open or closed to new ideas, the recital of personal faithstories will challenge and convict them in a contagious way.

Value of Faithstories

First century believers valued the power of personal/collective faithstories. They relied on such pictoral stories to turn the then-known world upside down, expanding the Kingdom of God. Rambo notes:

> Conversion stories touch the lives of people in ways that theological reflection rarely does. The tradition of conversion stories is derived, at least in part, from the Book of Acts in the New Testament. The conversions of Paul, Cornelius, the Philippian jailer, and Lydia point to the personal impact of religious change (1993:159).

Consider the following reasons why faithstories have such wide geographical, electrifying impact on their hearers.

Well-articulated faithstories challenge the five common myths that surround storytelling (Chapter 7). Believers tell their faithstories for more than entertainment purposes; they tell them to adults as well as children; they communicate them in urban centers as well as rural. While the storytellers may not be professional storytellers, they feel compelled to tell them anyway. By doing so, they connect Bible stories, personal experiences, and theology.

Well-articulated faithstories invite hearers to interact and dialogue with characters in a nonthreatening manner. Rather than alienate listeners through polemic debates or apologetics, faithstories tend to tease listeners into the dialogue. Such dialogue often challenges worldview distortion. It dares family, friends, and foes to intellectually, pictorially, and emotionally consider the validity of the testimony. Who can argue with the personableness of someone's faithstory? The blind man's faithstory provides an excellent case-in-point.

Well-articulated faithstories can deepen existing friendships, build new ones, or cause separations and divisions. When people tell others the intimate details of how life and faith intertwine, they open themselves up for rejection; they also offer listeners two cherished gifts— friendship with themselves as well as the Friend of friends, Jesus Christ. Some will reach out for the extended hand of friendship; others will turn their backs.

Well-articulated faithstories often become repeated by those not experiencing a faith-allegiance change to Christ. Mark illustrates: "Those tending the pigs ran off and reported this in the town and countryside....Those who had seen it told the people what had happened to the demon-possessed man—and told about the pigs as well" (Mk. 5:14,19). Faithstories, because of their earthiness, often become public stories. Telling stories spawns stories.

Well-articulated faithstories tie the past and future to the present. They eclipse time, making it possible for the stories of Old Testament Israelites and New Testament believers to impact any generation at any time (Hauerwas 1981:128). Such historical stories provide today's mariners with lighthouses and safe harbors in which to drop anchors. They also serve as worldview critiques, challenging mariners to accept personal/collective responsibility for past, present, and future actions.

Closely related to the last point, well-articulated faithstories connect evangelism to follow-up, resulting in a distinct community of faith. When new communities of faith begin to form, the faithstories of novice believers create new terminology, providing word symbols that become standard inclusions in narratives, songs, and literature (Hefner 1993:86,112). They exhibit certain kinetics and intonations that will become benchmarks to qualify future members. They define time in relation to conversion: a point, a process, a process/point/process, and so forth. Those who story their faith articulate theology formally. They may also develop an assimilation ritual to introduce new members into the community of faith, e.g. the requirement of new converts to articulate their faithstory before other members. And they provide opportunity over time to clarify and modify Christianity for themselves and others.

Well-articulated faithstories tie saving faith, daily faith, and community faith together (Rom. 15:4; 1 Cor. 10:11; Col. 2:6). But they go further; they tie one's personal faithstory to the Christian community-of-faith's story to Jesus Christ's story to Israel's story to Abraham's story to Adam & Eve's story. Faithstories solidify and socialize group members not only at a local level, but also at a universal level (Eph. 2:19-22).

Weaknesses of Faithstories

Faithstories have a downside as well as an upside. Over time, believers tend to develop "Christianese," i.e. a language understood only by insiders. Some examples would include: "walking in the Spirit," "praying through," "having your QT," "ask Jesus into your heart," "born again," "I feel led," "I have an unspoken request," and so forth. The same terminology used to create solidarity and to socialize new members can also cause outsiders to feel separated, even alienated. When communicating with unbelievers, storytellers must make a conscious effort to use terminology that is comprehensible.

Faithstories can diminish Christ's preeminence. Individual stories that glorify physical healing and/or the acquisition of material blessings, sordid past activities, or alleged total freedom gained from past temptations can focus the spotlight on the storyteller rather than Christ. Whether intuitively or intentionally, when this happens, the Storybook and the Storyline take a subservient role to the storyteller. Fackre shares this concern when he writes:

> One instance is an evangelism that wallows so extensively in *my* feelings, *my* decision, and *my* salvation that attention is drawn to things that happen to me rather than the divine happenings. Story-telling is, first and foremost, the biography of God, not my autobiography. It is an account of what "he" has done, is doing, and will do. Only in a modest and derivative sense is it concerned about our appropriation of these gracious actions (1973:14).

Storytellers must be alert to the potential danger of telling faithstories that exalt themselves rather than Jesus Christ; their faithstories should portray honesty and humility, pointing listeners to the Story of stories, Jesus Christ—not the recipients of his grace.

Faithstories can create competition and cause spiritual defeat. After hearing certain faithstories, some will wish they had lived a more despicable life so they could present such a stimulating testimony. Others will feel they will never be able to live up to the standard conveyed in the faithstory. Storytellers must be careful how they smith faithstories for these stories in turn smith the storytellers, the listeners, and most importantly, the God they intend to convey to others.

Conclusion

Due to the sacrificial work of Jesus Christ, the gospel stands finished. Because numerous lost mariners continue to traverse the open seas of life in search of a safe spiritual harbor, telling the story remains an unfinished task; telling faithstories connects to and continues a powerful tradition established by the first-century believers to expand the Kingdom of God. From their faithstories would emerge countless other faithstories from around the world, for as Rambo points out, "Every story of conversion calls for a conversion, confirms the validity of conversion, and shapes a person's experience of conversion" (1993:159).

Which recital model will work best? Should the storyteller use the recital of ideas and images? Events and characters? Faithstories? Some combination of these? To answer these questions, the storyteller must have the wisdom of the Holy Spirit and an intricate knowledge of the storyland.

To tell a story or series of stories that communicate effectively and challenge worldviews from God's perspective will require some smithing. The following chapter will consider how to smith a faithstory or a series of Bible stories.

Reflection:

What new questions does this chapter raise for you?

What do the variations of Paul's faithstory in Acts tell us?

Do you teach or story your faithstory?

What does your church do to intentionally train believers to tell their faithstories with confidence?

What ministry changes do you anticipate making?

For Further Reading:

Brereton, Virginia Lieson
    1991   From Sin to Salvation: Stories of Women's Conversions, 1800 to the Present. Bloomington, IN: Indiana University Press.
Fisk, Samuel
    1994   More Fascinating Conversion Stories. Grand Rapids, MI: Kregal Publications.
Hauerwas, Stanley
    1981   A Community of Character: Toward a Constructive Christian Social Ethic. Notre Dame: University of Notre Dame Press.
Pederson, Les, ed.
    1980   Missionary Go Home? Chicago: Moody Press.
Rambo, Lewis R.
    1993   Understanding Religious Conversion. New Haven: Yale University Press.

6
The Storysmith

To be relevant to the listener, faithstories or Bible stories must be contextualized. To remain accurate biblically, faith stories or Bible stories must reflect the sacred Storybook. These efforts require a certain type of person—a storysmith. A storysmith is a person gifted to design a singular story or a series of stories in such a way that they become context-specific, yet remain accurate biblically. This chapter will explore the unique role of the storysmith.

Forming a Storyteam

Designing stories that respect the sacred Storybook and the people who hear the stories requires some prior effort. Chapter 2 noted the role of the storyanalyst in relation to ascertaining the anthropological, theological, pedagogical, and curricular perspectives of the story in relation to three storylands. This role precedes the role of the storyteller.

Another role that precedes the role of storyteller, particularly in crosscultural settings, is the storysmith (see Figure 8 below). Developing effective faithstories or a series of Bible stories requires a team effort. A storyteam is needed. This team is comprised of a group of people, nationals and expatriates, driven by a singular vision to produce stories that relate to the target audience, yet demand worldview transformation. Team members would include, among others, storytellers, storyanalysts, and storysmiths. Some of these roles, no doubt, will overlap in individual members of the team, but it should not come as a surprise that all roles may not reside in one individual.

S T O R Y T E A M

Storyanalysts ⇨ *Storysmiths* ⇨ *Storytellers*

Figure 8. Towards effective storytelling

Smithing Faithstories

Preparing faithstories so that they communicate effectively to others will require homework. The greater the cultural distance, the greater the effort required. Not only must storytellers think how Christianity impacted their lives, they must also think how well the story will connect with the mariner's worldview (storylands). To illustrate, Paxtun women living in eastern Afghanistan and Pakistan's northwestern province will respond best to faithstories that highlight misfortunes, such as the death of a husband, mother or father, having no brothers or sons, raising children, not getting married, leaving mother at marriage:

> Among the Paxtun, these stories of grief or sadness (gham) are a valid medium of exchange, through which relationships are formed and maintained....Performing these rituals of grief and suffering largely defines what it means to be an honorable Paxtun woman....The main ingredient of a good story is gham (sadness)....beautiful stories that make you cry (Grima 1992:12).

Many Japanese will respond well to faithstories that emphasize how the storyteller joined the family of God rather than made an individual decision for Christ. For cultures that frown upon directness and confrontation but reward harmonious relationships, such faithstories come across as being credible. Faithstories that include episodes of the storyteller's ancestors will also bring credibility to those who define family to include past generations. No matter what the cultural distance, storytellers must smith their faithstories for maximum effect.

When writing one's lifestory, B.J. Hateley (1985) suggests that the writer describe life as a river, identifying the various tributaries that feed it. The author includes such tributaries as family, food, occupation, money, heroes, health, sexual development, death, loves of your life, hates of your life, moral development, time, meaning of your life. Some of these universal categories (and others) should prove helpful when preparing one's faithstory. The key question for the storysmith is *which?*

Those who analyze their faithstories from the anthropological (AL), theological (TL), pedagogical (PL) and curricular (CL) perspectives go a long ways in producing context-specific faithstories. After writing or taping and transcribing faithstories, a number of things can be done to compare them with the worldview of the people group targeted. For example, (1) underline the various values that drive it (AL), (2) identify the people and issues that influenced them to make a faith-allegiance change (AL, TL), (3) circle the components of the Storyline included (TL), (4) identify how Satan twisted the truth to keep them from becoming a believer (AL, pedagogical leg [PL], TL), (5) identify what non-issues by-passed them, i.e. those things the sacred Storybook considers important, but they did not (TL). For example, significant nonissues for the Ifugao would include such topics as hell and separation from God because of sin.

Other questions could include: What brought resolution (AL, TL)? Did they emphasize the past, present, future, or some combination (AL, PL, CL)? How did they sequence their faithstory into episodes (PL, CL)? How did people react to their faith-allegiance change? What kept their new faith-allegiance going in the midst of critique and persecution (AL, TL, CL)?

From the above exercise, a storysmith could then identify the potential tributaries that feed the river of life of the mariner. He or she can then smith the faithstories, keeping in mind the mariner's worldview, values, and social environments. The storysmith will want to focus on the timeless divine happenings that connect the faithstories to the life tributaries of the mariner, his or her family and community, and the community of faith (AL, PL, CL).

One of the most difficult things for storysmiths to do is to design faithstories in such a way that they get storied rather than taught. It seems so much easier to outline systematically aspects of faithstories, especially the section of the Storyline of Christ, and then teach rather than story. In that most of the messenger's former training supports a teaching approach to relate faithstories, he or she must make a conscious effort to change former habits so that teachers become storytellers. [1]

Boomershine provides storytellers with a helpful plan for learning to story faithstories:

- Read aloud
- Memorize sounds (verbs, repeated words)
- Identify the episodes (storywalk through the story sections)
- Tell it: to yourself, God, partner; get it off the page so it becomes a part of you
- Make hieroglyphics
- Repeat story in blocks
- Add gestures (1988).

The storytellers should practice the smithed faithstories till they feel comfortable. Then it's time to find some mariners. It's time to invite

> people into these stories as the definitional story of our life, and thereby authorizing people to give up, abandon, and renounce other stories that have shaped their lives in false or distorting ways....to reimagine our lives in these narrative modes (Brueggemann 1993:10).

Smithing A Story Series

Smithing a story series follows many of the same principles used in smithing faithstories. An analysis of the four legs of the story from the three perspectives of messenger, message, and mariner remains. The storyteam considers this study foundational as do they the job analysis (see Table 3). Storysmiths will seek to produce a storyboard that provides an adequate foundation for the gospel, incorporates the oft overlooked questions in evangelism, and ties evangelism to follow-up, all in a culturally relevant way that will challenge the mariner's worldview (Chapter 4). They can design the story series for a single storyteller or a team of storytellers.

Because of the great number of stories in the sacred Storybook, the storysmith must select those stories that accomplish their purpose, and when possible, speak directly to the mariner. The storysmith will establish the purpose by writing a series goal and specific objectives that cover the protagonist, antagonist, plot, conflict, and resolution. The series goal could read:

> Upon the completion of this series the Ifugao should desire a relationship with a personal God who defeated Satan and resolved the sin issue that separates the two parties, all through the death, burial, and resurrection of Jesus Christ, appropriate by faith the work of Jesus Christ, and demonstrate to others culturally appropriate transformed behavior.

Once the storyteam agrees to the series goal, specific objectives based off the series goal will follow:

Word: Admit that the Bible, God's Word, is superior to tradition for daily life and practice.

Table 3

Curriculum Checklist

Curriculum ✓ List

	Completed
Getting started	
1. Request Holy Spirit involvement	_____
2. Assemble curriculum team	_____
3. Conduct job analysis	_____
4. Conduct cultural analysis:	
Themes	_____
Decision-making	_____
Mode of communication	_____
Series goal and objectives	
1. Write series goal and objectives	_____
2. Write lesson goal and objectives	_____
3. Check levels of learning	_____
Selection of stories	
1. Determine time frame for series	_____
2. Determine total number of stories	_____
3. Select stories based on goal/objectives & cultural themes	_____
Sequence of stories	
1. Sequence foundational stories	_____
2. Insert connecting stories	_____
Exegesis of stories	
1. Identify setting, characters, plot, unifying themes, choices and changes	_____
2. Identify key theological points of emphasis	_____
3. Identify cultural bridges	_____
4. Identify cultural barriers	_____
5. Identify cultural gaps	_____
Development of individual lessons	
1. Identify discourse features	_____
2. Identify mode of communication	_____
3. Break up into episodes	_____
4. Check for cultural illustrations	_____
5. Check review format	_____
6. Check for cultural applications	_____
7. Check for theme unity	_____
8. Identify hidden curriculum	_____
Closure	
1. Conduct summatative evaluation	_____
2. Publish and disseminate	_____
3. Praise God for what has and will happen	_____

God: Acknowledge the God who created the Ifugao is
         more powerful than the ancestors, spirits, and
         Satan.
         Analyze why God's holiness prevents the Ifugao
         from communicating with God freely.

Satan: Identify Satan as the originator of all sin and the
         father of all unbelievers.
         Assess Satan's domination over the world system
         and its resulting effect on the Ifugao.
         Desire to avoid God's impending judgment of
         Satan and all those who follow him.

Ifugao: Acknowledge that personal / collective sin is the
         cause of spiritual separation from God.
         Define the Ifugao's part in the great conflict now
         being fought between God and Satan.
         Appropriate Jesus Christ as God's provisional
         substitute for salvation from sin.
         Rejoice in the new relationship with God through
         faith in Christ.
         Demonstrate culturally relevant transformed
         behavior.
         Accept God's unconditional love in providing a
         Substitute for sin.

        Once the storysmith determines the series goal and
objectives, he or she will ask several questions to
determine the length of the series: (1) How many times (be
realistic) will the mariner be willing to meet with the
storyteller(s)? One time a week for six weeks? Two times a
week for twelve weeks? and (2) How much solid Bible
background does the mariner have? The answers to these

questions will inform the storysmith as to the number of stories that the series can cover realistically.

The above questions also assure that process takes precedence over precanned programs. The storysmith can offer mariners a story series limited to their time frame, not that of the team. Should the mariner demonstrate interest after the completion of the story series, possibly he or she will commit to another short series. The storysmith could then build the second series based off of the first.

Selection of the specific Bible stories follows. The storysmith may need to select two types of stories (depending on the total number): foundational and connecting. Foundational stories refer to those stories that meet the series goal, fulfilling one or more of the specific objectives. Connecting stories refer to those stories added to maintain seamless continuity between the foundational stories.

The storysmith can now sequence the stories. To do this, he or she will design the sequence in such a way that it aids subsequent follow-up as well as present evangelism. Placing the foundational evangelism stories in chronological order, when possible, will help the mariner grasp the historical development of the sacred Storybook, as well as the Storyline. To maintain the flow of the Storyline they will insert connecting stories or needed information (so and so died, a number of years passed and this happened). Should the series contain numerous stories, the storysmith will divide the series into the number of clusters that reflect the mariner's understanding of numbers, e.g. the number four from a Native American perspective (wholeness) versus that of some Asians (death).

Exegeting the individual stories follows. The storysmith will identify the setting, plot, unifying themes, choices, and changes for each story. He or she will also isolate the key theological components of the gospel that the storyteller(s) will emphasize in the story. Team members will then discuss potential cultural barriers, bridges, and knowledge gaps in relation to the total exegesis project. Should the research demonstrate a nonmatch between the specific objectives and the story selected (except for connecting stories), they will search for another story.

Having identified previously the mariner's discourse features and preferred mode of communication, the storysmith will write the individual lessons. He or she will break the story down into manageable episodes, add illustrations, call for review and application, all in a culturally relevant format. Once a story is complete, the storysmith will search for hidden curriculum (worldview and value biases of the storyteam) inserted into the lesson. Hidden curriculum includes, among others, the type of questions included (those that emphasize the individual or the group), the lesson sequence and sections included promote a certain hermeneutic, the amount of participation called for by the teacher as well as the seating arrangement (circular or rows) reflects views of empowerment and community. The storysmith will also check the individual lessons for theme unity. The individual lessons represent small sections of the big picture, forming a seamless web (see Figure 9).

Storytellers can now go to work. After internalizing a story, they must remember to story it to the mariner, not summarize the plot or tell about it. Telling the story will unleash the power of narrative. It also produces time-tested curriculum as storytellers evaluate individual stories as well as the story series (Steffen 1993b). The storytellers

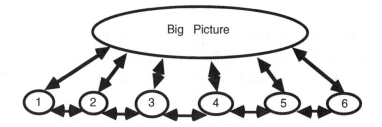

Figure 9. Checking for the seamless big picture

can then feel satisfied with the published curriculum they disseminate. In conclusion, the storyteam will want to praise God again for all that has happened and will happen because of the tested story series.

Conclusion

Comprehended stories are contextualized stories. Storysmiths play a major role in making the connection between teller and hearer become a reality. They recognize that good storytelling does not begin with telling stories; rather it begins with analysis, followed by smithing, and then, telling. Effective storysmiths take the time necessary to create stories that communicate and challenge.

Building a storyteam comprised of storyanalysts, storysmiths, and storytellers will require overcoming a number of myths that surround storytelling. Chapter 7 will discuss some of the myths that mitigate against the use of stories in ministry.

[1] The National Storytelling Association can provide helpful networks and principles, as well as the Network of Biblical Storytellers (E-mail: nobsint@aol.com).

Reflection:

What new questions does this chapter raise for you?
What job descriptions would be necessary for a storyteam?
What gifts and talents would a storysmith require?
Does the lesson series format promote discussion and life
    transformation?
What ministry changes do you need to make?

For Further Reading:

Boomershine, Thomas E.
    1988   Story Journey: An Invitation to the Gospel as Storytelling.
            Nashville: Abingdon Press.
Ford, LeRoy
    1991   A Curriculum Design Manual For Theological Education.
            Nashville, TN: Broadman Press.
McIlwain, Trevor
    1993   Firm Foundations: Creation to Christ. Sanford, FL: New
            Tribes Mission.
Slack, Jim and J.O. Terry
    1994   Chronological Bible Storying: A Methodology for
            Presenting the Gospel to Oral Communicators. Richmond,
            VA: Southern Baptist Convention, Foreign Misson Board.

7
Miffing the Myths

Just because we lack imagination is
no reason to think that the ancients did.
AMOS WILDER

One-third of the way into the semester in a classroom at a renowned American seminary, one group of students composed of various ethnic backgrounds, including Anglos, Asians, African-Americans, found themselves doing quite well. They could follow the professor's linear thought patterns and handle the assignments appropriately.

Another group of students did not find the course as user-friendly. While they enjoyed the course, they found the professor's linear, sequential lectures not only difficult to follow, but often downright boring. One particular assignment finally brought the submerged problem to the surface.

The assignment required the students to interact with class materials, focusing exclusively on the facts. The professor discouraged the use of personal pronouns or anecdotal material. In short, the students were to separate the facts from the framework.

The second group of students chafed under such rigid restrictions. They were puzzled as to how anyone could separate the facts from the framework. Life, as they perceived it, was an organized whole, not a host of isolated parts. They envisioned life as a plate of chop suey with all the ingredients stirred together so as to unleash all the distinctive flavors as they interact with each other, not a plate of steak, potatoes, and peas separated into distinct servings (Chang 1984).

This case study raises a number of pertinent questions for Christian workers who wish to teach others. Who in the audience benefits most from studying under a linear teacher? A holistic teacher (one who presents the big picture)? Which listeners must conduct mental gymnastics to be able to comprehend what the teacher teaches? How well can they communicate to others what they heard? Why do Christian workers tend to place the greatest emphasis on the cognitive domain to the virtual exclusion of emotions and feelings? Whatever happened to stories? On a more personal level, *how user-friendly is your teaching style?*

I recently perused a conference notebook used in the 1994 North American Conference for Itinerant Evangelists. Of the approximate 90 plenary, seminars and workshops offered during the conference, no title contained the words "narrative" or "story." The closest titles to these words included "drama" and "talk shows." The same could be said of outlines provided by the speakers. Why do we often overlook storytelling as a viable evangelistic/teaching tool?

Could storytelling, a universal form of communication that connects the mind, the heart, and emotions, be an effective communication tool not only to facilitate comprehension but also to communicate with minimal content corruption? What baggage keeps Christian workers from using more stories in their teaching?

A number of myths surround the use of stories, not only in the classroom but in numerous other public and private arenas. Such myths can kill our desire to learn, stifle creativity, suffocate emotions, smother holistic thinking, choke imagination, give the impression that stories lack value, or discourage us from using stories in ministry or academia. The case study above points out one such myth—stories are synonymous with fiction. Therefore, stories have no role in "real" education. Such a myth can easily damage effective communication and kill learning. Here are five such myths that surround stories.

☞ Myth 1: Stories are for entertainment

Some people understand stories to be separated totally from reality (see Table 4 below). Storytelling, or watching or listening to stories, is something one does for fun. It is something one does alone or with friends to kick back and relax, to have a good time. In short, stories entertain.

While stories certainly deal with fiction, some go far beyond it. Stories can also speak about the realities of life. In fact, stories identify who we are as individuals, a social class, a people group, a nation, a world. Should any of these entities not have a story, it stands without an identity. Without an identity, hopelessness tends to prevail. Stories give people hope and security because they provide an identity.

Names provide another insight into the reality of stories. What is in a name? Stories! Real stories! Stories (names) perpetuate ideas and ideals, both positive and negative. That is, of course, unless the name is forgotten. But ongoing storytelling assures that names remain alive. Remember Hitler? Gandhi? Esther? Saddam? Mother Teresa? Alexander the Great? Martin Luther King? Paul? Mary? Scrooge? Stories keep the memories of people (names) alive, and, thereby, provide continually "living" models to follow or avoid.

Stories create, maintain, and change worldviews. People express beliefs and behavior based on stories heard from parents, relatives, strangers, friends, and enemies. Stories influence how a person views and participates in the world. Stories are much more than fiction. They are symbols of reality because they create and shape reality; they are values and philosophy articulated.

Stories tie reason, emotions, and imagination together. They weave together the fabric of life, interlacing facts and framework. Such tapestry makes communication and learning a natural process. Rather than by-passing the mind, as some think stories do, stories involve the total person. This healthy contribution of storytelling may be missed by some because of a closely related second myth.

☞ Myth 2: Stories are for children

During childhood, stories play an integral role in personal development. I remember my mother reading to us before bedtime when I was a boy. While I certainly never grasped the author's deeper intent behind such characters as Huck Finn, Jim, Pap, Widow Douglas, Miss Watson, Tom Sawyer, Aunt Polly, Becky Thatcher, Injun Joe, Sid, Muff Potter, Mary, Judge Thatcher, or Joe Harper,

I definitely experienced life as the characters knew it. I boldly rode the raft down the mighty Mississippi. I felt mud ooze between my toes. I trembled as I watched grave robbers do their evil work. I joined these bigger-than-life characters vicariously.

I also remember stories from Sunday School. Through Bible stories, skilled (and sometimes not so skilled) teachers pulled me into the lives and ancient times of people such as Moses, Cain and Abel, Caleb, the spies and Rahab, Balaam and his donkey, Jezebel, Jonah and the fish, Martha, Peter, Onesimus, and the Sons of Thunder. I began to learn about the God behind these people (and animals), and what he expected of them, all of which molded my developing worldview.

There were also summertime stories. The local library hosted special times for children to listen to stories. I rarely missed such occasions because I knew every reading provided a new, mysterious journey—and I had a free ticket to join that journey. I lived for stories. Yes, stories certainly are made for children.

Then I attended grade school and high school to gain an education. Sometime during those years the use of stories got lost. Part of the developmental process into mature adulthood seemed to include the extraction of stories. History became facts, dates, and places rather than human stories. I began to lose interest in history, and any other subject that separated abstract concepts from concrete realities. Schooling became a necessary chore.

I went to school again to train for missions. Among other things, I learned about word studies and objective, systematic theology. Well-defined abstract categories, based on thorough exegesis of words, provided a complete picture of God and Christianity applicable for the entire world. The Bible became, for me, a theological handbook. I built my library accordingly. More layers of adult "wisdom" covered up the life-engaging stories of my childhood.

Mark Shaw's intriguing book, *Doing Theology with Huck & Jim,* attempts to reconcile story (concreteness) and theology (abstractness). To accomplish this, Shaw begins each lesson with a story from a childhood classic or popular culture. The story is followed with theological commentary as the author highlights the "Theology Behind the Story."

Behind Shaw's strategy seems to lie the assumption that we must first "speak to the child within with whimsical parables and stories" to gain access "to the basic beliefs and values that might otherwise be denied" (1993:12). Once accomplished, "The commentary section speaks to the 'adult' within us, making possible mature understanding and mature decisions based on biblical truth" (ibid., p.12). One wonders if Shaw has fallen into the same trap I experienced during my education journey, i.e. stories are for children while theology is for adults.

For those trained to think in a linear fashion, Paul's epistles rightfully become favorite watering holes. Unlike Jesus' more holistic teaching, they often find Paul's linear letters easier to comprehend, outline and relate to others. They find themselves drawn naturally to this logical section of Scripture.

Paul claimed that when he became a man he put away childish things. It seems some interpret this to mean Paul gave up childish stories for adult theology. As an adult, he could now advance to a higher level of cognition. He therefore replaced stories with abstract, propositional, timeless theology. Could anyone reading Romans disagree?

But Miller astutely observes, "Even Romans must not be read as simply an abstract propositional statement of truth. The book is best understood within the story of Paul's missionary journey" (1987:128). As noted in Chapter 3, Witherington (1994) would agree: Pauline theology cannot be accurately understood without first grasping the stories that precede it. Paul certainly strove to keep propositions in intimate contact with the stories that produced them. Paul never outgrew his need for stories, nor did his readers. Has the Enlightenment torpedoed the hermeneutics of evangelicals?

Yes, stories are for children, including all the children of God, no matter what the biological age. When Jesus warns, "unless you change and become like little children," he was talking about attitude towards God and simple trust in him, not learning styles. Arguing that stories are for children rather than adults "denies the intelligence and sophistication of both." Adults never outgrow the need for stories.

☛ Myth 3: Stories are for those living outside urban areas

There are those who argue (sometimes snobbishly) that stories are for those living outside of urban areas. It has long been recognized that tribal and peasant people rely heavily on stories in order to socialize succeeding generations. Having no libraries to store knowledge, every member of society becomes a walking library. When death takes a community member, valuable stories become lost forever. Figuratively, a library burns to the ground. That is, unless the deceased comes back to life figuratively through the stories conveyed to others in, for instance, stories of work, relationships, religion, nation building, parenting, or a host of other topics. Most likely, this transfer of knowledge has happened because it is an expected societal norm. The old are to socialize the young through example and story.

The Ifugao tribal people of the Philippines reintroduced me to stories. In our seven years of living among the Ifugao, I spent literally hundreds of hours listening to stories about the Flood, countless gods and ancestors, land disputes, farming, animal husbandry, hunting trips, typhoons, animal sacrifices, and W.W. II exploits. Certain stories would be retold over and over. While this made language learning ideal, it called for a major adjustment of my teaching style. My theological handbook Bible failed to impress the Ifugao. I learned firsthand the sanctity of stories among tribal people.

A move to metro Manila continued my education about stories. I soon learned that urban Filipinos have a passion for stories that rivaled that of the Ifugao's. Societal or geographical differences did not change the love for stories. Just as rural integrated communities relied on stories to socialize, educate and entertain, so did urban segmented communities. While some media (TV, VCRs, comics) differed in some geographical areas of the Philippines, storytelling remained number one.

Back in the USA, reality-based TV has become extremely popular. Shows such as *60 Minutes, 20/20, Inside Edition, Cops, Saturday Night Live, Rescue 911, The Oprah Winfrey Show,* MTV's *The Real World,* and the numerous soaps and talk shows testify to this fact. An introductory line from one reality-based program provides educators with a possible clue as to the "why" of its popularity: "Real stories of the Highway Patrol." Television (and videos), through dramatized life narrations, connect well with a growing number of baby boomers, baby busters, and various cultures.

In relation to Baby Busters, experts argue that storytelling is a powerful communication tool for teaching the United States' first post-Christian generation. Leighton Ford, who ministers to Generation Xers, stresses the power of narrative preaching, particularly stories that focus on Jesus and personal stories that make the storyteller vulnerable (Ford 1994; Tapia 1994). Urbanites have not outgrown the need for stories.

☛ Myth 4: Only professional storytellers can tell stories

Anyone who has heard professional storytellers practice their trade may readily accept this myth. Professional storytellers have the innate ability to pull listeners into a contrived environment, surrounded by a cast of characters. Time seems to stand still as the plot unfolds. Listeners soon find themselves siding with certain characters, while reacting to others. They may cry, curse, scream in terror, laugh, or sit puzzled or dazed. Whatever the response, the storyteller has succeeded again in capturing the very soul of the listener. In essence, the storyteller adds a new, invisible member to the cast.

While few of us may be professional storytellers, all of us tell stories. After work or school we tell our spouse or friends what happened during the day. When the police officer stops us for a violation we tell our story. At club meetings we swap stories, including the one with the police officer. When relationships break down we tell our story to whoever will listen. After a sporting event we tell stories about the muffs and miracles. All events produce storytellers. The world moves because people tell stories.

While not all believers may be professional storytellers, Scripture encourages all to be storytellers. One such story they must tell, wherever the gospel goes, surrounds the lavish gift bestowed on Jesus. Mary anointed Jesus' head with expensive perfume worth a year's wage. This sacrificial action evidenced her acceptance of the King's impending death, in spite of the unbelief of the Disciples. The gospel writer assumes Christian workers will relate this intriguing story of Mary's convincing faith around the world.

Believers have the privilege to tell an even greater story, the story of Jesus Christ. As witnesses in a court of law testify before the judge and jury what they know about a case, so believers are to testify to family, friends, and strangers around the world what they know about Jesus Christ. Those possessing the gift of evangelism may be more "professional" at the assignment than those without it. Nevertheless, *every* believer can tell the story of Jesus Christ to others. And *all* can improve their storytelling capabilities.

☛ Myth 5: Bible stories and theology are unrelated

Some Bible teachers feel that telling Bible stories wastes valuable teaching time. They would rather move a lesson directly to the heart of the matter—theology. That Bible stories may contain or relay theology on their own often goes uninvestigated.

Telling a story and telling about a story are as different as telling about a particular ethnic group and living among them. Telling a story requires listeners to interact with the characters and reach conclusions. The

Table 4

Five Story Myths That Kill

☞ Myth 1: Stories are for entertainment
☞ Myth 2: Stories are for children
☞ Myth 3: Stories are for those living outside urban
 areas
☞ Myth 4: Only professional storytellers can tell
 stories
☞ Myth 5: Bible stories and theology are unrelated

---

conclusions may or may not agree with those of the storyteller.

Telling about a story provides the storyteller opportunity to interpret the story for the listeners. This avenue can provide the storyteller much more predictable lesson outcomes.

Some teachers begin lessons with a Bible story to hook the audience, and then quickly move to exegete the theology from the story. They then recast the theological content from story to systematic theology. For example, a teacher may exegete the abstract doctrine of love your neighbor from the story of the Good Samaritan and develop the concept systematically. Mixing learning styles, of course, can be very helpful for linear thinkers, and should therefore be utilized in such contexts. But this is not necessarily true for holistic thinkers initially.

If Bible teachers can exegete theology from stories, it would seem theology preexists in the stories. McLuhan (1973) would agree when he argues the message is the medium because the message is imbedded in the medium. Storytelling is much more than a communication medium; it *is* the medium. When a Bible teacher exegetes theology from a story, he or she is exchanging teaching mediums, not message content. The question becomes, Which medium best communicates the message? Not, Which medium possesses theology? Tilley's argument rings true: "If stories give meaning to the metaphors / stereotypes / code words / doctrines which we use, then a narrative theology is more fundamental than a propositonal theology"(1985:11). Stories do not just illustrate theology, like the Pentateuch, they *are* theology.

Madeliene L'Engle argues, "Jesus was not a theologian. He was God who told stories." If Jesus relied on parabolic stories to communicate his message, does this not imply theology lies resident in the stories? Holistic thinkers would argue it does. The myth that claims theology must be extracted from stories and systematized to be valid theology must be challenged.

Conclusion

Many other myths surround the story genre. These, along with the five myths identified above, have the debilitating ability to kill effective communication and learning. One should never believe all the stories heard about stories.

While an effective ministry cannot be built and perpetuated solely on storytelling, it cannot be done effectively without it. The final chapter will provide readers with seven reasons why stories should be sanctioned in ministry, not silenced.

Reflection:

What new questions does this chapter raise for you?

What other myths would you add?

What ministry changes do you anticipate making?

For Further Reading:

Chang, Peter S. C.
   1984   "Steak, Potatoes, Peas and Chopsuey—Linear and Non-Linear Thinking" *In* Missions & Theological Education in World Perspective. Harvie M. Conn and Samuel F. Rowen, eds. Farmington, MI: Associates of Urbanus, pp.113-123.
Ford, Kevin
   1995   Jesus for a New Generation: Putting the Gospel in the Language of Xers. Downers Grove, IL: InterVarsity Press.
Ford, Leighton
   1994   The Power of Story: Rediscovering the Oldest, Most Natural Way to Reach People for Christ. Colorado Springs, CO: NavPress Publishing Group.
Tapia, Andres
   1994   Reaching the First Post-Christian Generation. Christianity Today. 38(10): 18-23.

8
Why Tell Stories?

Bree said, "And now, Tarkheena, tell us your story. And don't hurry it—I'm feeling comfortable now." Aravis immediately began, sitting quite still and using a rather different tone and style from her usual one. For in Calormen, story-telling (whether the stories are true or made up) is a thing you're taught, just as English boys and girls are taught essay-writing. The difference is that people want to hear the stories, whereas I never heard of anyone who wanted to read the essays.
C.S. LEWIS

My developing skills in the Ifugao language and culture finally made public teaching possible. I enthusiastically developed a number of Bible lessons that followed the topical outline we received in pre-field training: the Bible, God, Satan, humanity, sin, judgment, and Jesus Christ. Once listeners were introduced to the authority-base (the Bible), I quickly moved on to the second part of the outline (God), and so forth. I presented the lessons in a topical, systematic format. My goal was not only to communicate the gospel, but to communicate it in such a way that the listeners could effectively articulate it to others.

But as I taught, I soon realized that the Ifugao found it difficult to follow the topical presentations, and found it even harder to explain the content to others. I was astonished and perplexed.

Some changes were necessary, so I added a number of stories from the Old Testament to illustrate the abstract (theoretical) concepts in the lessons through pictoral (concrete) characters and objects (e.g., creation, the fall, Cain and Abel, the flood, the escape from Egypt, the giving of the Ten Commandments, the Tabernacle, Elijah and Baal). The response was phenomenal. Not only did the evangelistic sessions come alive, the recipients became instant evangelists, telling the stories to friends enthusiastically. From then on I integrated stories in all my evangelistic efforts.

Storytelling has become a lost art for many Christian workers. As discussed in the previous chapter, a number of hollow myths raise questions about the purpose or usefulness of stories. For example, stories should target children because they provide excellent entertainment. Adults eventually outgrow the need for stories, replacing them with the more sophisticated objective, propositional thinking. In that character derives from dogmas, creeds, and theology, never waste time telling stories. As a result of these and other related myths, Christian workers have often unwittingly set aside storytelling. To help reconnect God's stories to evangelism-discipleship, I will highlight seven reasons why storytelling should become a skill practiced by all Christian workers.

1. *Storytelling is a universal form of communication.* No matter where one travels in this world, people love to tell and listen to stories. Age does not deter this desire. Whether young children, teenagers, or senior citizens, all enjoy entering the life experiences of others through stories.

Whatever the topic discussed, stories often become an integral part of the dialogue. Whether used to argue a point, interject humor, illustrate a key insight, comfort a despondent friend, challenge the champion, or simply pass the time of day, a story has a unique way of finding its way into the conversation.

Stories can be heard anywhere. One can hear stories in church, the court house, the movie theater, the home, the bus, the car, the locker room, prison, or on a walk in the woods. Geographic location does little to deter the flow of stories.

Not only do all people tell stories, they have a need to do so. This leads us to the second reason for storytelling.

2. *More than half of the world's population prefer the concrete mode of learning.* According to Barrett (1997), the illiterates and semi-literates in the world probably outnumber literates. People with such backgrounds tend to express themselves more through concrete forms (stories and symbols) than abstract concepts (propositional thinking and philosophy).

A growing number of Americans prefer the concrete mode of communication. This is due, at least in part, to a major shift in communication preference. One of the reasons behind this shift (and the dropping literacy rate) is the television. With the average TV sound bite now around 13 seconds, and the average image length less than 3 seconds (often without linear logic), it is no wonder that those under its daily influence have little time or desire for reading which helps develop and reinforce linear thought. Consequently, newspaper businesses continue to dwindle while video production companies proliferate. If Christian workers rely too heavily on evangelism and teaching strategies based upon abstract, literary foundations, argues Klem (1982), two-thirds of the world may be by-passed.

3. *Stories connect with our imagination and emotions.* Effective communication touches not only the mind, it also touches the heart and emotions. One of the best modes of communication to accomplish this is the story.

While stories provide dates, times, places, names, and chronologies, they simultaneously produce tears, cheers, fear, anger, confidence, defensiveness, conviction, sarcasm, fantasy, despair, and hope. Stories draw listeners into the lives of the characters (people, animals, or objects, real or fictitious). Listeners (participants) not only hear what happened to such characters; through the imagination they vicariously enter the experience. Schneidau eloquently captures this point when he states: "stories have a way of tapping those feelings that we habitually anesthetize" (Schneidau 1986:136).

People appreciate stories because they mirror their total lives of fact and feeling. Stories uniquely interweave reason, mystery, and reactions, causing listeners to reflect on personal / group beliefs and actions. Stories unleash the imagination, making learning an exciting, life-changing experience.

4. *Every major religion uses stories to socialize its young, convert potential followers, and indoctrinate*

members. Buddhism, Islam, Hinduism, Judaism, Christianity—all use stories to expand (and limit) membership, assure ongoing generational conversion, and bring disciples to maturation. Whether Paul was evangelizing Jews or Gentiles, the audience heard relevant stories. Unbelieving Jews heard about cultural heroes, such as Abraham, Moses, and David (Acts 13:13-43). Unbelieving Gentiles heard about the powerful God behind the creation story (Acts 14:8-18; 17:16-34). Maturing believers heard the same stories with a different emphasis.

All major religions use stories to differentiate true members from false, acceptable behavior from unacceptable. Stories create community. Could one of the reasons for this be that stories provide an inoffensive, nonthreatening way of challenging basic beliefs and behavior?

5. *Approximately 75 percent of the Bible is narrative*. Figure 10 depicts the three basic styles of literature that dominate the landscape of the Scriptures: narrative, poetry, and thought-organized format. The narrative sections are predominant. Writers over the centuries have documented the actions of a host of characters: from kings to slaves, from those who follow God to those who live for personal or collective gain, from animals to objects. Such stories serve as mirrors to reflect our own perspective of life, and more importantly, God's. Koller astutely points out:

> The Bible was not given to reveal the lives of Abraham, Isaac, and Jacob, but to reveal *the hand of God* in the lives of Abraham, Isaac, and Jacob; not as a revelation of Mary and Martha and Lazarus, but as a revelation of *the Savior* of Mary and Martha and Lazarus (1962:32).

Poetry covers approximately 15 percent of the sacred text. Songs, lamentations, and proverbs provide readers and listeners with a variety of avenues to express, and to experience deep inner emotions. These portions of Scripture demonstrate the feeling side of people (affective domain), and the God behind such emotions.

The thought-organized format comprises the remaining 10 percent. The apostle Paul's Greek-influenced writings fall under this category, where logical, linear thinking tends to dominate. Interestingly, many westerners schooled in the tradition of the Greeks (including myself) prefer to spend the majority of time in the Scripture's smallest literary style. If God communicated the majority of his message to the world through stories, what does this suggest to Christian workers?

The reader will notice I note the above percentages are approximate. It is very difficult to isolate the exact percentages of the various genres, especially since most (all?) Bible authors incorporate ingeniously several genres within their writings. For example, notice the use of poetry set in a narrative context in Isaiah or other prophets (see NIV translation). Why is it that Bible authors chose to communicate their contribution to the sacred Storybook in multi-genres, most often framed in narrative?

6. *Stories create instant evangelists.* People find it very easy to repeat a good story. Whether the story centers around juicy gossip or the gospel of Jesus Christ, something within each of us wants to hear and tell such stories. Suppressing a good story is like trying to resist a jar full of one's favorite cookies. Sooner or later, the temptation becomes too strong. The cookie gets eaten; the story gets told. Told stories get retold.

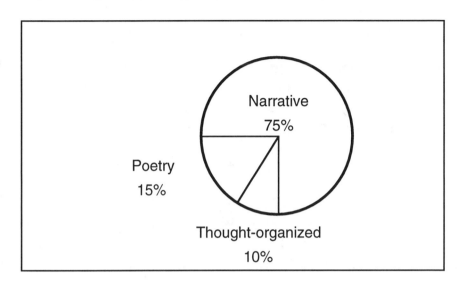

Figure 10. Major literary styles of the Bible
(Steffen 1993b:117)

Because the Ifugao could relate well to the life-experiences of Bible characters, they not only applied the stories to their lives, they immediately retold them to family and friends, even before they switched faith allegiance to Jesus Christ. Stories create storytellers.

7. *Jesus taught theology through stories.* It is interesting to note that Jesus never wrote a book on systematic theology. Yet, he taught theology wherever he went. As a holistic thinker, Jesus often used parabolic stories to tease audiences into reflecting on new ways of thinking about life.

As Jesus' listeners wrestled with new theology introduced innocently yet intentionally through parabolic stories, they were challenged to examine traditions, form new images of God, and transform behavior. To remain content with past realities became uncomfortable; yet to take up Jesus' challenges to step out of the boat, taste new wine, display the golden lampstands, turn from family members, extend mercy to others, search for hidden objects, and donate material goods and wealth to the poor was not a comfortable choice either. Whichever direction the listeners took, they found no middle ground. They had met God. Jesus' stories, packed with theology, caused reason, imagination, and emotions to collide; demanding a change of allegiance. Jesus' example demonstrates forcibly that stories can communicate theology effectively.

Conclusion

The Bible begins with the story of creation and ends with a vision of God's recreation. Peppered generously between *alpha* and *omega* are a host of stories. While stories dominate the Scripture landscape, they rarely enter the Christian worker's evangelism-discipleship strategies intentionally. Leland Ryken cogently asks:

> Why does the Bible contain so many stories? Is it possible that stories reveal some truths and experiences in a way that no other literary form does — and if so, what are they? What is the difference in our picture of God, when we read stories in which God acts, as compared with theological statements about the nature of God? What does the Bible communicate through our imagination that it does not communicate through our reason? If the Bible uses the imagination as one way of communicating truth, should we not show an identical confidence in the power of the imagination to convey religious truth? If so, would a good startpoint be to respect the story quality of the Bible in our exposition of it (1979:38)?

Is it not time that today's Christian workers revitalize one of the world's oldest, most universal arts—storytelling? Such revitalization will not only increase communication between Christian workers and audiences, but will also increase storytelling as members of the community of faith repeat the stories to family and friends.

Reflection:

What new questions does this chapter raise for you?

What other reasons would you add to this list?

What ministry changes do you anticipate making?

For Further Reading:

Boomershine, Thomas E.
    1988   Story Journey: An Invitation to the Gospel as Storytelling.
            Nashville: Abingdon Press.
Grant, Reg and John Reed
    1990   Telling Stories to Touch the Heart: How to Use Stories to
            Communicate God's Truth. Wheaton, IL: Victor Books.
Stallings, James O.
    1988   Telling the Story: Evangelism in Black Churches. Valley
            Forge: Judson Press.

Conclusion

Reconnecting God's Story to Ministry seeks to reconnect the story genre of Scripture to evangelism and follow-up. Why have so many Christian workers, including myself, overlooked the fundamental genre God chose to deliver his Word to the world? If God had consulted me in my earlier years of ministry as to how best to complete Operation World, I would have made at least the following practical suggestions:

- Provide people a completed Bible. Why waste 1200 years to write and compile it?
- Don't waste 30 years for Jesus to grow up; have him come as an adult.
- Don't confuse people with parabolic stories; just give them the bare, minimal facts, in a systematic format.
- Provide people an abbreviated pamphlet on the life of Jesus presented in four abstract, logical, linear laws.

For some reason God does not give time the same emphasis many of us place on it. Relationships and community take precedence over time and task. Foundation receives as much (more?) attention as follow-up. Emotions do not take a back seat to facts, nor does confrontation to contextualization. Characters define abstract concepts and add to our theological categories of convenience. Logic comes in many cultural packages. Bible narratives contain deep theological truths. And as Brueggemann (1993) points out, "The wonder is that these old texts as models of alternative imagination do indeed continue to have that generative, transformative capacity, even in our time and place" (p.11).

The Holy Spirit's example as Storysmith and Jesus' example as Storyteller provides models for all Christian workers. If these two members of the Trinity relied so heavily on the magnetic and memorable narrative genre, can we afford to do less? For most readers this may demand a number of paradigm shifts. In relation to evangelism-discipleship these shifts may come in a variety of stages:

- from legal laws to
  faithstory *and* legal laws to
  faithstory that *integrates* the legal laws;
- from *little if any* foundation for the gospel to
  a *solid foundation* for the gospel;
- from *little connection* between foundation and
  follow-up to a *continuum* that leaves fewer
  surprises for the new disciple;
- from *surface* relationships to *deep*
  relationships;
- from *linear logic* to *circular logic;*
- from *little contextualization* to
  context-specific stories.

The journey required to make the necessary paradigm shifts, no matter how long it takes, is well worth the effort. Just as it helps locate the messenger's place in God's historical narrative, so it does the same for the mariner. While it encourages all believers, including those without the gift of evangelist, to participate in telling the greatest story ever told, it offers the mariner transcendence and transformation. The power and poetry released in stories make it much harder for people to go to hell. Is it not time to get serious about telling faithstories and Bible stories that communicate and challenge? Is it not time to reconnect God's stories, including our faithstories, to ministry?

Glossary

Abstract   defining or describing something theoretically, i.e. apart from visible objects.

Cognitive styles   the multiple ways in which people learn, store, and retrieve information.

Concrete   defining or describing something pictorially.

Faithstory   the story of how one comes to know Jesus Christ as Savior.

Genre   artificial designations which attempt to classify literary styles.

Holistic   providing a global, big picture perspective.

Linear   the communicator presents a topic in a logical, sequential manner.

Mariner   a mariner can be defined as an unbelieving member of a people group adrift spiritually on the seas of life in search of a safe harbor in which to drop the anchor of faith. These individuals have a "God-shaped vacuum;" their heart, says St. Augustine, "is restless, until it repose in Thee."

Messenger   a believer-follower of Jesus Christ.

Message   the good news of Jesus Christ.

Mode of communication   ways by which people communicate.

Narrative   "...the account by a narrator of events and participants moving in some pattern over time and space" (Fackre 1984:5).

Paradigm shift   a change in the fundamental rules and regulations by which things are normally done to address or solve problems.

Propositional truth objective theological truths categorized from Scripture that tend to be seen as universals, therefore fixed and nonnegotiable.

Storyanalyst a person gifted to analyze the worldviews, values, and social environments of the storyteller, people groups of the Bible, as well as the people group targeted for Christ.

Storybook the Holy Bible.

Storylands the worldviews, values, and social environments of the storytellers, the people groups of the Bible, and the people groups targeted for Christ.

Storyline the good news pertaining to life, death, burial, resurrection, and ascension of Jesus Christ in relation to restoring our broken relationship with God.

Storysmith a person gifted to design a singular story or a series of stories in such a way that they become context-specific, yet remain accurate biblically.

Storyteam a group of people driven by a singular vision to produce stories that relate to the target audience, yet demand worldview transformation. Team members will include, among others, storyanalysts, storysmiths, and storytellers.

Supracultural need the need of a Savior to restore a broken relationship with God due to inherited and practiced sin.

Story "An account of characters and events in a plot moving over time and space through conflict toward resolution" (Fackre 1984:5).

Worldview the linguistic-cultural assumptions and presuppositions founded and maintained by myths and stories that distinguish one people group / subculture from another.

Bibliography

Arias, Mortimer
1984   Announcing the Reign of God: Evangelization and the
        Subversive Memory of Jesus. Philadelphia: Fortress Press.
Bailey, Kenneth E.
1976   Poet and Peasant: A Literary-Cultural Approach to the
        Parables in Luke. Grand Rapids, MI: Eerdmans.
1983   Through Peasant Eyes: A Literary-Cultural Approach to
        the Parables in Luke. Grand Rapids, MI: Eerdmans.
1992   Finding the Lost: Cutural Keys to Luke 15. St. Louis, MO:
        Concordia Publishing House.
Barna, George
1993   Today's Pastors. Ventura, CA: Regal Books.
Barr, David L.
1987   New Testament Story: An Introduction. Belmont, CA:
        Wadsworth Publishing Company.
Barrett, David B.
1997   Annual Statistical Table on Global Mission: 1997.
        International Bulletin of Missionary Research. 21(1): 24-25.
Baxter, J. Sidlow
1966   Explore the Book: A Basic and Broadly Interpretive Course
        of Bible Study From Genesis to Revelation. Grand Rapids,
        MI: Zondervan Publishing House.
Bellah, Robert N. et al.
1985   Habits of the Heart: Individualism and Commitment in
        American Life. New York: Harper & Row, Publishers.
Bertaux, Daniel, ed.
1981   Biography and Society: The Life History Approach in the
        Social Sciences. Beverly Hills, CA: Sage Publications.
Boomershine, Thomas E.
1988   Story Journey: An Invitation to the Gospel as Storytelling.
        Nashville: Abingdon Press.
Brereton, Virginia Lieson
1991   From Sin to Salvation: Stories of Women's Conversions,
        1800 to the Present. Bloomington, IN: Indiana University
        Press.
Brueggemann, Walter
1977   The Land: Place as Gift, Promise, and Challenge in Biblical
        Faith. Philadelphia: Fortress Press.

1993   Biblical Perspectives on Evangelism: Living in A Three-Storied Universe. Nashville, TN: Abingdon Press.

Chang, Peter S. C.
1984   "Steak, Potatoes, Peas and Chopsuey—Linear and Non-Linear Thinking" *In* Missions & Theological Education in World Perspective. Harvie M. Conn and Samuel F. Rowen, eds. (Farmington, MI: Associates of Urbanus), pp.113-123.

Clancy, M.T.
1993   Memory to Written Record. Cambridge: Blackwell Publishing.

Dyrness, William A.
1983   Let the Earth Rejoice!: A Biblical Theology of Holistic Mission. Westchester, IL: Crossway Books.
1989   How Does America Hear the Gospel? Grand Rapids, MI: Wm. B. Eerdmans.

Eisenhower, William D.
1995   Why Should the Devil Have All the Good Stories? Paper presented at the meeting of the Evangelical Theological Society meetings, Philadelphia, PA., Nov.16-18.

Fackre, Gabriel
1973   Do and Tell: Engagement Evangelism in the '70s. Grand Rapids, MI: Wm. B. Eerdmans.
1975   Word in Deed: Theological Themes in Evangelism. Grand Rapids, MI: Wm. B. Eerdmans.
1984   The Christian Story: A Narrative Interpretation of Basic Christian Doctrines. Grand Rapids, MI: Wm. B. Eerdmans.

Fee, Gordon D. and Douglas Stuart
1993   How To Read the Bible for All its Worth: A Guide to Understanding the Bible. Grand Rapids, MI: Zondervan.

Fisk, Samuel
1994   More Fascinating Conversion Stories. Grand Rapids, MI: Kregal Publications.

Ford, Kevin
1995   Jesus for a New Generation: Putting the Gospel in the Language of Xers. Downers Grove, IL: InterVarsity Press.

Ford, Leighton
1994   The Power of Story: Rediscovering the Oldest, Most Natural Way to Reach People for Christ. Colorado Springs, CO: NavPress Publishing Group.

Ford, LeRoy
1991   A Curriculum Design Manual For Theological Education. Nashville, TN: Broadman Press.

Gilfillan, Berin
　　1996　Video Training Opens Huge Possibilities in the Third
　　　　　World. Global Church Growth: Strategies for Today's
　　　　　Leaders. 32(4): 8-9.
Grant, Reg and John Reed
　　1990　Telling Stories to Touch the Heart: How to Use Stories to
　　　　　Communicate God's Truth. Wheaton, IL: Victor Books.
Grima, Benedicte
　　1992　The Performance of Emotion Among Paxtun Women: The
　　　　　Misfortunes Which Have Befallen Me. Austin: University
　　　　　of Texas Press.
Hateley, B.J.
　　1985　Telling Your Story, Exploring Your Faith: Writing Your
　　　　　Life Story for Personal Insight and Spiritual Growth. St.
　　　　　Louis, MO: CBP Press.
Hauerwas, Stanley
　　1981　A Community of Character: Toward a Constructive
　　　　　Christian Social Ethic. Notre Dame: University of Notre
　　　　　Dame Press.
Hauerwas, Stanley and David Burrell
　　1989　From System to Story: An Alternative Pattern or Rationality
　　　　　in Ethics *In* Hauerwas, Stanley and L. Gregory Jones, eds.
　　　　　Why Narrative? Readings in Narrative Theology. (Grand
　　　　　Rapids, MI: Wm. B. Eerdmans), pp.158-190.
Hauerwas, Stanley and L. Gregory Jones, eds.
　　1989　Why Narrative? Readings in Narrative Theology. Grand
　　　　　Rapids, MI: Wm. B. Eerdmans.
Hefner, Robert W., ed.
　　1993　Conversion to Christianity: Historical and Anthropological
　　　　　Perspectives on a Great Transformation. Los Angeles:
　　　　　University of California Press.
Hesselgrave, David J.
　　1978　Communicating Christ Cross-Culturally: An Introduction to
　　　　　Missionary Communication. Grand Rapids, MI: Zondervan
　　　　　Publishing House.
　　1994　Scripture and Strategy: The Use of the Bible in Postmodern
　　　　　Church and Mission. Pasadena, CA: William Carey Library.
Hesselgrave, David J. and Edward Rommen
　　1989　Contextualization: Meanings, Methods, and Models. Grand
　　　　　Rapids, MI: Baker Book House.
Hiebert, Paul G.
　　1976　Cultural Anthropology. Philadelphia: J.B. Lippincott
　　　　　Company.

1985   Anthropological Insights for Missionaries. Grand Rapids, MI: Baker Book House.

1995   Incarnational Ministry: Planting Churches in Band, Tribal, Peasant, and Urban Societies. Grand Rapids, MI: Baker Book House.

Houston, Tom
1993   Dangerous Days for Evangelism. Evangelical Missions Quarterly, 29(3): 258.

Keener, Craig S.
1995   The IVP Bible Background Commentary: New Testament. Downers Grove, IL: InterVarsity Press.

Kelber, Werner H.
1983   The Oral and the Written Gospel. The Hermeneutics of Speaking and Writing in the Synoptic Tradition, Mark, Paul, and Q. Philadelphia: Fortress Press.

Klem, Herbert, V.
1982   Oral Communication of the Scripture: Insights From African Oral Art. Pasadena, CA: William Carey Library.

Koller, Charles W.
1962   Expository Preaching Without Notes. Grand Rapids, MI: Baker Book House.

Kraft, Chrales K.
1991   Communication Theory for Christian Witness. NY: Orbis Books.

Larson, Donald N.
1978   The Viable Missionary: Learner, Trader, Story Teller. Missiology: An International Review. 6(2): 155-163.

Lewis, C. S.
1952   Mere Christianity. N.Y: Macmillan.
1956   The Horse and His Boy. N.Y: Macmillan.

Lingenfelter, Sherwood G.
1992   Transforming Culture: A Challenge for Christian Mission. Grand Rapids, MI: Baker Book House.

1996   Agents of Change: A Guide for Effective Cross-Cultural Ministry. Grand Rapids, MI: Baker Book House.

Lingenfelter, Sherwood G. and Marvin K. Mayers
1986   Ministering Cross-Culturally: An Incarnational Model for Personal Relationships. Grand Rapids, MI: Baker Book House.

Mayers, Marvin K.
1987   Christianity Confronts Culture: A Strategy for Crosscultural Evangelism. Grand Rapids, MI: Zondervan Publishing House.

McClendon, James Wm. Jr.
  1974   Biography as Theology: How Life-Stories Can Remake
         Today's Theology. Nashville, TN: Abingdon Press.
McDowell, Josh
  1979   Evidence That Demands A Verdict. San Bernadino, CA:
         Here's Life Publishers.
McIlwain, Trevor
  1987   Building on Firm Foundations: Guidelines for Evangelism
         and Teaching Believers, Vol. 1. Sanford, FL: New Tribes
         Mission.
  1993   Firm Foundations: Creation to Christ. Sanford, FL: New
         Tribe Mission.
McLuhan, Marshall
  1973   Understanding Media: The Extention of Man. London:
         Abacus.
Metz, Johann Baptist
  1989   A Short Apology of Narrative *In* Stanley Hauerwas and L.
         Gregory Jones, Why Narrative? Readings in Narrative
         Theology. (Grand Rapids, MI: Wm. B. Eerdmans), pp.251-
         262.
Midgett, Linda
  1993   The Emerging Sunday-school Avant-Garde. Christianity
         Today. 37(1): 45.
Miller, Donald
  1987   Story and Context: An Introduction to Christian Education.
         Nashville: Abingdon Press.
Niebuhr, H. Richard
  1989   The Story of Our Life *In* Hauerwas, Stanley and L. Gregory
         Jones, eds. Why Narrative? Readings in Narrative
         Theology. (Grand Rapids, MI: Wm. B. Eerdmans), pp.21-
         44.
Ong, Walter J.
  1981   The Presence of the Word: Some Prolegomena for Cultural
         and Religious History. Minneapolis, MN: University of
         Minnesota Press.
  1982   Orality and Literacy: Technologizing of the Word. New
         York: Methuen.
Patterson, George and Richard Scoggins
  1993   Church Multiplication Guide: Helping Churches to
         Reproduce Locally and Abroad. Pasadena, CA: William
         Carey Library.
Pederson, Les, ed.
  1980   Missionary Go Home? Chicago: Moody Press.

Powell, Mark Allan
  1990   What is Narrative Criticism? Minneapolis, MN: Fortress
         Press.
Pratt, Richard L., Jr.
  1990   He Gave Us Stories: The Bible Student's Guide to
         Interpreting Old Testament Narratives. Brentwood, TN:
         Wolgemuth & Hyatt, Publishers, Inc.
Rambo, Lewis R.
  1993   Understanding Religious Conversion. New Haven: Yale
         University Press.
Ryken, Leland
  1979   The Bible: God's Story-book. Christianity Today, 23(23):
         34-38.
  1984   How to Read the Bible as Literature. Grand Rapids, MI:
         Academie Books.
  1987   Words of Delight: A Literary Introduction to the Bible.
         Grand Rapids, MI: Baker Book House.
Ryken, Leland and Tremper Longman, III, eds.
  1993   A Complete Literary Guide to the Bible. Grand Rapids, MI:
         Zondervan Publishing House.
Saucy, Robert L.
  1993   The Case for Progressive Dispensationalism: The Interfaith
         Between Dispensational and Non-Dispensational
         Theology. Grand Rapids, MI: Zondervan Publishing House.
Schneidau, Herbert N.
  1986   Biblical Narrative and Modern Consciousness *In* Frank
         McConnel, ed. The Bible and the Narrative Tradition. (New
         York: Oxford University Press), pp. 132-150.
Shaw, Mark
  1993   Doing Theology with Huck & Jim: Parables for
         Understanding Doctrine. Downers Grove, IL: InterVarsity
         Press.
Shea, John
  1978   Stories of God: An Unauthorized Biography. Chicago:
         Thomas Moore Press.
Slack, Jim and J.O. Terry
  1994   Chronological Bible Storying: A Methodology for
         Presenting the Gospel to Oral Communicators. Richmond,
         VA: Southern Baptist Convention, Foreign Misson Board.
Stallings, James O.
  1988   Telling the Story: Evangelism in Black Churches. Valley
         Forge: Judson Press.

Stiles, J. Mack
  1995   Speaking of Jesus: How to Tell Your Friends the Best News
          They Will Ever Hear. Downers Grove, IL: InterVarsity
          Press.
Steffen, Tom A.
  1993a   Don't Show the Jesus Film... Evangelical Missions
          Quarterly. 29(3): 272-275.
  1993b   Passing the Baton: Church Planting That Empowers. La
          Habra, CA: Center for Organizational & Ministry
          Development.
  1995   Storying the Storybook to Tribals. International Journal of
          Frontier Missions. 12 (2): 99-104.
Stewart, Edward C. and Milton J. Bennett
  1991   American Cultural Patterns: A Cross-Cultural Perspective.
          Yarmouth, ME: Intercultural Press, Inc.
Swartley, Willard M.
  1994   Israel's Scripture Traditions and the Synoptic Gospels.
          Peabody, MA: Hendrickson Publishers, Inc.
Tapia, Andres
  1994   Reaching the First Post-Christian Generation. Christianity
          Today. 38(10): 18-23.
Tilley, Terrence W.
  1985   Story Theology. Collegeville, MN: The Liturgical Press.
Tonkin, Elizabeth
  1992   Narrating Our Pasts: The Social Construction of Oral
          History. (Studies in Oral and Literate Cultures: No. 22).
          N.Y: Cambridge University Press.
VanderWerff, Lyle
  1994   Mission Lessons From History: A Laboratory of
          Missiological Insights Gained from Christian-Muslim
          Relationships. International Journal of Frontier Missions.
          11(2): 75-79.
Wells, David F.
  1993   No Room for Truth: Or Whatever Happened to
          Evangelical Theology? Grand Rapids, MI: Zondervan
          Publishing House.
Witherington, III, Ben
  1994   Paul's Narrative Thought World: The Tapestry of Tragedy
          and Triumph. Louisville, KY: Westminster/John Knox
          Press.